T0326604

HOW AMERICA WAS TRICKED ON TAX POLICY

HOW AMERICA WAS TRICKED ON TAX POLICY

SECRETS AND UNDISCLOSED PRACTICES

DR. BRET N. BOGENSCHNEIDER

*"We don't pay taxes. Only
the 'little people' pay taxes."*
Leona Helmsley

ANTHEM PRESS

Anthem Press
An imprint of Wimbledon Publishing Company
www.anthempress.com

This edition first published in UK and USA 2020
by ANTHEM PRESS
75–76 Blackfriars Road, London SE1 8HA, UK
or PO Box 9779, London SW19 7ZG, UK
and
244 Madison Ave #116, New York, NY 10016, USA

British Library Cataloguing-in-Publication Data
A catalogue record for this book is available from the British Library.

Library of Congress Cataloging-in-Publication Data
Library of Congress Control Number: 2020936296

ISBN-13: 978-1-78527-427-5 (Hbk)
ISBN-10: 1-78527-427-9 (Hbk)
ISBN-13: 978-1-78527-430-5 (Pbk)
ISBN-10: 1-78527-430-9 (Pbk)

This title is also available as an e-book.

CONTENTS

INTRODUCTION: THE CLASSIC DECEPTIONS IN TAX POLICY

You've probably been told many things about tax policy:

- That the wealthy pay a surplus of tax into the system and that workers somehow draw out these funds disproportionately to receive a net benefit.
- That the economy will grow quickly because of tax cuts for large corporations that supposedly give those companies enough free cash to make investments into new business lines.
- That if the wealthy were asked to pay taxes they might simply pack up and leave, creating a loss to the economy.

Of course, none of these claims are true. The truth is, what you have been told about tax policy is a trick designed to deceive you into working ever longer hours and paying taxes at ever higher effective rates. Many of these and other ideas about taxes and tax policy, especially those that you hear on television, are inconsistent with each other and make little or no logical sense. For example, if the first idea were true, that the wealthy pay copious amounts of surplus tax into the system, then it cannot also be true that the wealthy would leave if they were forced to pay any tax.

At this early stage, you should be at least suspicious that something is amiss with what you've been told about tax policy. The truth is that tax policy is formed by and through a series of deceptions. The foremost deception, which is the premise of both economic and philosophical thinking on taxation, is that it is always better for society that workers pay the bulk of taxes and that the wealthy and large corporations pay as little as possible. Economists claim that this type of tax policy is efficient for society. However, any supposed efficiency gains could arise only if the wealthy have very special plans for capital that they could achieve if they were not required to pay taxes. In fact, there are good reasons to believe that workers are better able to efficiently allocate small amounts of capital they have earned through work. The act of engaging in productive work is strong evidence that a person should be able to find a productive use for some capital. This means that it would be better and more *efficient* for society if taxes on the persons that engage in productive work were reduced from current levels so workers could invest their own capital, derived from their own work, in various productive pursuits. The productive pursuits of workers might be expected to yield efficiency gains for the economy including enhanced small business formation. Such productive efforts are encouraged where workers are not forced to pay nearly all of their surplus capital over to the government in the form of high rates of labor taxes and small business taxation. Some might even go further and call that a "fair" approach to tax policy.

Notably, the Social Security Trust Fund, as accumulated over the years from withholding taxes on prior generations of workers, was used to fund the federal budget, until even it ran out of money. All the while, politicians claimed, preposterously, that workers don't pay taxes and that the wealthy pay a disproportionate amount of taxes because of the progressivity of the income tax system. Even a cursory glance at the federal budget reveals that such a claim is sheer nonsense, however. If we look to cash flows, the reality is that workers remit the bulk of the taxes through income taxes, employment taxes, sales taxes, gasoline taxes, property taxes, excise taxes, governmental fees for licenses and on and on. Since most of these tax types are either regressive (such as employment taxes) or not progressively indexed (such as property taxes), the overall system of taxation is regressive as workers pay a higher proportion of their earnings into tax types other than income taxes. The wealthy do not pay proportionate amounts largely because capital income is not taxed currently and the non-indexed tax types, such as sales taxes, are simply not as material to the wealthy in dollar terms as they are to workers. If we apply a more reasonable accounting method to tax policy and take into accounting holding gains on capital assets as tracked by the Federal Reserve, for example, then the *effective tax rates* on the wealthy are about one-third (1/3rd) those paid by the working classes. As will be explained in further detail later, it turns out that effective tax rates are more important than statutory tax rates or marginal tax rates and even the underlying methods of calculating an effective tax rate have been manipulated to deceive working taxpayers.

Yet, the progressivity of the income tax is the issue of tax policy that you see most often discussed on television. Of course, the wealthy as a class are indeed most concerned about the progressivity of *income taxation* because that is the tax which they predominantly pay. Yet, that hyper focus on income taxation is an illustration of a type of trick or, in some cases, may represent even a bona fide mistake, such as where the television tax commentator may fail to realize that employment or property taxes, as examples, are onerous to persons that do not have high incomes by which to pay these sorts of taxes. In any case, the Social Security Trust Fund cash so accumulated by the toil and sweat of generations of past workers has now been depleted, which will lead eventually to a governmental cash flow crisis as current workers cannot realistically be expected to pay any more in taxes than they already do.

Partly as a result of tax policies designed not to tax capital very much, the fortunes of the wealthy today are so vast that it requires a stretching of the imagination to see how any one person could efficiently allocate so much capital into productive investments. The allocation of large amounts of capital—say, a billion dollars—into productive investments is a very difficult task, so difficult that many wealthy individuals do not even attempt to allocate capital efficiently. Rather, the wealthy often channel largely untaxed capital into huge mansions or palaces, yachts, private aircraft and so on. Jeff Bezos was recently reported to have built a mansion with 25 bathrooms, as a prime example.[1] These sort of expenditures are not productive investments and are designed merely to maximize creature comforts; they do not generate any economic return to society besides the initial act of production, and this enhancement of comfort means very little in economic terms. Contrary to what you may have been led to believe, it is not economically "efficient" for society to simply produce and consume comfort items that do not yield any economic return.

If taxes on workers and small business were reduced to more manageable levels, some workers would be clever enough to allocate small amounts of capital into productive activities like farms, restaurants or other small businesses that would generate an ongoing economic return and make society better off. I used to think that the diffusion of small amounts of capital among lots of Americans was a key aspect of the American dream and that capital diffusion helped to explain why the United States was such a successful and prosperous nation. The politicians who have designed the tax system, though, clearly don't share these ideas about capital diffusion and economic policy. Tax policy more and more is meant to force workers to pay most of the taxes in order to concentrate capital into a few hands and thereby facilitate the accumulation of vast fortunes by the wealthy. As they have always done throughout history, the modern-day wealthy then continue to deploy the capital into building pleasure palaces of various sorts that do not yield any economic return.

Tax proposals to reduce taxes for workers and small businesses, such as that developed later in this book, represent the opposite of current economic and moral theorizing on tax policy. Quite amazingly, however, nearly all the empirical evidence available on tax policy supports a reduction of taxes on *work* as a means of increasing economic growth. As will be explained further, it is fair to call this the *scientific view* on tax policy, as it is based on the available evidence. Economic theory is generally not based on evidence. It may surprise you that there is little or no data or other empirical evidence to support the various tax policies proposed by so-called economic experts who call for tax cuts for the wealthy and large corporations. But there isn't. The deeper you dig into tax policy, the less substance you will find. The object of tax scholarship really is to keep the shovel out of your hands, and thus, to keep you quietly paying taxes through the direct withholding of funds out of your paycheck.

Meanwhile the wealthy and large corporations vociferously complain about taxes but pay almost nothing in relative terms. The corporate share of the tax base prior to the Tax Cuts and Jobs Act of 2017 was 9 percent but was trending sharply downward even before the tax cuts, and may now be as little as 1 percent or 2 percent.[2] The downward trend in corporate taxes was due in part to the lack of enforcement of the corporate tax laws by the government. For example, the Internal Revenue Service has adopted a variety of programs designed not to comprehensively audit large corporations as they do other smaller business and individual taxpayers. With further sharp reductions to the corporate statutory tax rate, the corporate share of the tax base has likely been reduced from 9 percent to much less. For comparison, the corporate share of the tax base ranged between 20 percent and 30 percent in prior decades. As the corporate share of the tax base is further reduced, workers will be expected to pay more taxes into the system to make up the difference, either now or in the future; the timing of when that happens depends, of course, on how quickly the federal system becomes insolvent.[3]

The foremost object of tax policy is accordingly to convince working taxpayers that the tax system is smart, fair and efficient when it is obviously not. The goal of this book is to reveal many of the deceptions that currently exist within tax policy. The deceptions you will read about in these pages are not so different from magic tricks. However, in this case, instead of believing a rabbit came out of a hat, taxpayers are fooled into believing that the tax system is either fair or efficient—it is in reality neither, nor is it intended to be so. The many philosophers who wish to debate the relative fairness of the tax system have missed the important point, which is that only the powerful are interested in debating whether the current tax system may be considered "fair." The working classes do not find this supposedly philosophical inquiry as to the "fairness" of wage and other types of taxation to be even a valid question and go about their lives under the assumption that the tax system is grossly and abjectly unfair. And, as will be explained, it turns out it is the workers and not the philosophers who are correct that relative fairness has little practical import or relevance to the design of tax policy.

Professional philosophers have largely failed to recognize that a method of accounting, consistently applied, is strictly necessary to reach moral conclusions about the fairness of the tax system. Insofar as many workers are only aware of a cash-basis means of accounting for tax payments, they have, by necessity, consistently applied that accounting method and reached the cogent conclusion that the tax system is not "fair" to them since workers plainly remit most of the taxes measured on a cash basis. Of course, various philosophers have encouraged the wealthy to believe that the tax system should be considered "fair" by creating special accounting methods to be creatively applied on a noncash basis within their own moral frameworks. These special accounting methods make it possible to say that the wealthy should be assumed to have paid a proportionate share of taxes to then allow for a supposed "redistribution" for basic needs in the "welfare state," as example. In any case, the results are thereby twisted to such a degree that some background in accrual accounting (or even forensic accounting) is helpful in attempting to apply the many special accounting methods of moral philosophy to tax policy. This will be explained further below.

The broader purposes of the overall tax system are better revealed by what is referred to as "postmodern" philosophy and are actually twofold: The first purpose is to collect tax nearly exclusively from workers by withholding directly out of their paychecks. The second purpose is to allow the wealthy to feel powerful by not paying much of anything in tax. This is often achieved as a result of what the wealthy consider "prudent" tax avoidance planning— yet, such means of rational tax avoidance are only made available to relatively wealthy persons under the tax laws. Both of these elements are absolutely necessary to the functioning and design of the current tax system. The American billionaire Leona Helmsley stated it best: "We don't pay taxes. Only the 'little people' pay taxes."[4] That is basically an accurate factual description of the tax system. Helmsley was a real estate heir and for long the richest person in the United States. Similar to Bezos's 25 bathrooms, Helmsley famously left $11 million in a trust fund for her dog upon her death. She captured in these few words the postmodern view of taxation and tax policy: The wealthy don't pay much tax relative to either their income or accumulated wealth and that the reason for this is that the wealthy are simply more powerful than the working class. The wealthy further view workers as "little people" and that is how the wealthy classes justify *to themselves* not paying much tax even though this is both economically inefficient and morally wrong.

THE CLASSIC DECEPTIONS

Now let us proceed to the analysis of the classic deceptions that are used to create tax policy. Please note that not a single one of the claims in this list is accurate or true:

Deception #1. Tax cuts for the wealthy will cause economic growth.

Deception #2. Large corporations are experiencing a cash shortfall that can be alleviated by cutting their taxes.

Deception #3. Capital is like a delicate hummingbird: It is mobile and will leave if subjected to tax.

Deception #4. By inventing a special way to count taxes, we conclude the wealthy pay significant amounts of tax (e.g., the top 1 percent pay roughly half of all taxes).

Deception #5. Statutory tax rates, not effective tax rates, are what's important to tax policy.

Deception #6. High business tax rates reduce economic growth by reducing the economic return on investment.

Deception #7. The working poor don't pay taxes because income tax rates are progressive.

Deception #8. There are no social costs to high taxes on workers.

Deception #9. Workers and poor people are cognitively inferior to the wealthy and unable to make rational economic decisions.

Deception #10. Tax cuts for large corporations are the only viable tax policy option and never tax cuts for small business.

Deception #11. Tax cuts for large corporations will reduce prices on consumer products.

The following sections lay out why every one of these statements is a deception, a trick played on taxpayers to ensure that the wealthy and corporations don't pay anything close to a proportionate share of the tax base.

Deception #1. Tax cuts for the wealthy will cause economic growth

Tax cuts for the wealthy will actually not lead to economic growth. This idea is not novel as it has indeed been tried before, time and time again, throughout human history. In reality, there is no empirical evidence that tax reductions for the wealthy cause economic growth or that lower tax rates for the wealthy foster economic growth. The bulk of the evidence suggests that the opposite is probably true.[5] Nearly all the empirical evidence on record indicates that higher levels of per capita gross domestic product (GDP) are associated with higher taxes. This is true both for cross-country comparisons and also over time within individual countries where the taxes have changed.[6] A few very small countries have established themselves as tax havens, including, for example, Ireland and Singapore, and these small countries are the exception in international tax policy and cannot be used as a guide to setting tax policy in larger countries; in essence, these tax havens have positioned themselves as parasites of other countries. In all other contexts, the empirical evidence indicates that higher taxes are associated with higher GDP in every country and in every historical period on record. So far, economists have not produced a sliver of evidence—not even a correlation between these variables of tax cuts and economic growth. The empirical evidence is so obviously to the contrary that it is rather silly to search for such a correlation where none exists. However, there are examples of tax increases on capital appearing to have directly caused spurts of economic growth, including in the implementation of the Tax Reform Act of 1986.[7]

A novel idea that has never really been tried before, except in Switzerland, which taxes wages relatively lightly,[8] is *not* taxing workers at high rates and seeing if that sort of progressive tax policy causes economic growth. I wish to propose that it is plainly obvious based on the available evidence that a tax cut for workers and small businesses would cause sustained economic growth. Ironically, such tax cuts for workers is the very tax policy that economists nearly unanimously counsel against. The wealthy have been able to escape taxes throughout history, and nothing about minimizing taxes for the wealthy and hoping for economic growth is a new policy idea. Exempting the wealthy from paying taxes has been done time and again and it seems to result in the building of lots and lots of fancy palaces and the acquisition of more and more creature comforts but not economic growth.[9]

Deception #2. *Large corporations are experiencing a cash shortfall that can be alleviated by cutting their taxes*

Although tax scholars and television and radio commentators constantly repeat the claim that corporate tax cuts cause economic growth, this simply makes no sense. Large corporations have been experiencing a cash surplus, not a cash shortfall.[10] In fact, large corporations have accumulated so much cash on their balance sheets that it threatens the stability of the economic system. The total amount of cash held on corporate balance sheets exceeded $3 trillion at the time of the drafting of this book.[11] Additional tax incentives to these firms should not be expected to cause economic growth—they should be expected to increase corporations' hoarding of cash to ever-larger amounts. Many large firms operate their businesses as an annuity, with the goal of drawing out as much cash as possible from the business without reinvesting capital.

If someday there does appear some empirical evidence that corporate tax cuts *do* cause economic growth, this would be attributable not to the availability of cash, but to how the tax cuts might enhance the optimism of corporate executives to make capital reinvestment. But, lots of economic policies apart from tax cuts could have a positive or negative impact on the optimism of corporate executives. Because nearly all economic activity is linked to consumer spending, tax cuts for consumers would seem more likely to increase consumer spending and to thereby increase the prospects of economic growth[12] as business spending might then increase to match the increase in consumer spending. The contrary economic idea that higher consumer spending might arise from corporate tax cuts to companies with ample surpluses of cash seems utterly unrealistic for many reasons. Large corporations have ready access to credit and even if they were short of cash could easily borrow money to fund incremental business investment. If large corporations are not making capital investments into the broader economy it really does not seem plausible to conclude this is a result of the lack of capital that must be alleviated through the tax system—the underlying idea just isn't plausible.

Deception #3. Capital is like a delicate hummingbird: It is mobile and will leave if subjected to tax

Many large corporations operate by harvesting profits by and through a dominant market position, where the business is operated like an annuity and the maximum amount of cash is drawn out from the operating business with the minimum amount of capital reinvestment. Such profit harvesting is best accomplished when the competition has been eliminated from the local market somehow. In economic terms, this market advantage is known as collecting economic "rents" out of the marketplace, and firms that engage in this are described as *rent-seeking* market behavior. One way to use tax policy to facilitate rent-seeking market behavior by large businesses is through granting preferential tax treatment to only large corporations. The benefits that the current tax system delivers to large corporations comes at the expense of small businesses in the marketplace by reducing the relative rate of economic return to these competitors. At one point, small businesses were competitors in the marketplace in various lines of business, but now are unable to make a profit after taking into account the relatively higher tax rates charged to small business in comparison to large business. Once the small businesses are out of the picture, the large corporations are positioned to provide a good or service in the absence of any competition and can charge whatever price they determine that consumers might be willing and able to pay.

The term "rents" is helpful here because corporate activity can be thought of like a landlord who wishes to collect rents from tenants. A good example is a Walmart superstore that serves a locality and has no competing local stores. Just like landlords are unlikely to stop being landlords if there is still some rent to be collected—that is, profit to be made, without regard to the tax rate—corporations are the same. This Walmart will leave the locality only when its market position has been eroded in some way and that erosion has reduced available profits (or "rents") to zero. This might occur if the Walmart is subjected to competition from another large grocery or retail chain, like Target or Kroger. Tax policy could have a negative impact on Walmart if, say, Target stores were exempted from various types of tax but Walmart stores were not. Such an unequal tax treatment would potentially erode the market position of one business at the expense of another. However, this rarely, if ever, happens to large corporations. In contrast, it is nearly always the case that small businesses are subjected to much higher tax rates than large corporations, so the tax system accrues to the benefit of large corporations and at the expense of small business. This makes it unlikely that corporate taxes have any effect on large corporations at all, and they certainly would not cause them to raise prices. Redesigning the tax system to foster competition in the marketplace might even lead to lower prices by increasing competition to large corporations in the marketplace and forcing them to compete with small businesses on price.

Large firms, especially after the Tax Cuts and Jobs Act of 2017, are generally taxed much less than small businesses; this rate differential reduces the after-tax rate of return to small business and ultimately assists large corporations in eliminating small businesses as competitors in the marketplace. Large firms may thus continue to enjoy monopolistic market conditions across the United States and increasingly in Europe and can extract rents from the marketplace to an extraordinary degree. An example is Starbucks, which now operates in many European cities with very low effective tax rates even though many local coffee shops in those same cities are subject to taxation on any profits at hefty European tax rates. Accordingly, it is rather outrageous to suggest that large corporations such as Starbucks might fly away like a delicate hummingbird from these market monopolies because of corporate tax. The hummingbird anal-ogy simply is not as pertinent to large firms as it might be to small ones. Large corporations are more like crocodiles than hummingbirds. Once they move into a body of water, they will stick around until they have completely exhausted all the food sources—that is, profits or rents. Not even levying a tax will make that crocodile move to a new river if there remains even one wildebeest or small coffee shop owner waiting to be consumed.

Deception #4. By inventing a special way to count taxes, we conclude the wealthy pay significant amounts of tax (e.g., the top 1 percent pay roughly half of all income taxes)

Several tax organizations operate tax policy websites that continuously publish reports that the rich pay lots of taxes. Often the claim is that the top 1 percent pay half of all US income taxes.[13] Another oft-quoted statistic is that 50 percent of the population pays 97 percent of the income taxes.[14] The implication is that because of the progressive tax rate structure of the federal income tax system that workers and lower-income workers do not pay as much in taxes as the wealthy. These organizations do not attempt to determine the source of federal tax receipts apart from current year income taxation that comprise the federal budget, however. Wage taxes, which are levied pursuant to a regressive rate structure (where a ceiling is applied and earnings above the ceiling are exempted from wage tax) are simply ignored by dropping the word *wage* before taxes and slipping in the word *income* as if that were a reasonable assumption in the formulation of tax policy. However, it's not a reasonable assumption. These tax policy organizations claim to be bipartisan—and that's true to some extent—as perhaps the only thing Republicans and Democrats agree on is that workers should fund as much of the tax base as possible. So, these organizations create misleading statistics that support the idea that the wealthy are remitting a disproportionate amount of the tax base through progressive federal income taxation, which just isn't true.

The reality of the federal budget is quite different from what you've been told by these tax policy organizations. The truth is this: A large portion of receipts arise from wage withholding in the form of Social Security and other taxes levied on workers, not from income taxes levied on the wealthy. The tax organizations that publish the misleading statistics are aware of this reality, so they need to create an explanation as to why only income taxes should count as federal tax receipts, rather than wage tax receipts, or federal government borrowing out of the Social Security trust fund, for example. In tax parlance, the invention of a new system of reporting on tax remittances comprises what is referred to as an "accounting method"; here, an accounting method for counting tax remittances to the Federal government. The misleading aspect of these tax statistics is that they do not consistently apply that special method of accounting. Then, absent consistency in counting taxes paid, it is possible to manipulate the statistical result to reach nearly any result.

One method of accounting applied as justification is to create (or to "book an accrual") an offsetting amount for hypothetical social benefits solely to workers to be received at some point in the future. However, this special accrual method is applied solely to workers as taxpayers. Anytime an offsetting amount is created or accrued based on a hypothetical for one group and not another group, it creates a fudge. For example, such a corresponding accrual for hypothetical economic benefits is then not accrued for large corporations or wealthy individuals in order to account for the similar benefits they receive from tax remittances. This means there is a mismatch within the application of the accounting for accruals or cash payments depending on whether the taxpayer is a worker versus a wealthy person or a large corporation. The mismatch in the accounting for future benefits represents the fudge, where it is really possible to create any possible result in tax policy by positing a future benefit of a greater or lesser amount. The result is then to say that tax remittances under the wage tax system are $0 (or even negative). The method is illustrated in the table that inserts a question mark to represent the fudge where one group of taxpayers follow one accounting method and another group follow a different accounting method:

	Current Taxes	**Future Benefits**	**Net Gain/(Loss)**
Worker	(45)	45	0
High income	(45)	?	?
Corporation	(9)	?	?

This mismatched method of accounting for wage taxes can be challenged in two ways. First, given the many accruals in the modern tax system, tax policy could instead proceed on what is referred to as a "cash-basis" method of accounting. On a cash basis, the amount of current remittances by workers is very high, and this level of remittance could be compared to payments made by other taxpayers, such as large corporations. This would be used to calculate an effective tax rate based on cash taxes in order to formulate a coherent tax policy by applying one and only one method of accounting in the respective analysis. Second, hypothetical future benefits could be posited to other taxpayers. If similar hypothetical benefits are counted today for both workers and other groups, then the result could or would change as it would be determined that workers are indeed paying net taxes. The failure to consider a cash-basis method of accounting to formulate tax policy is an egregious and astounding omission— no trained accountant could possibly overlook such an omission.

An additional sleight-of-hand is next applied by some television commentators and tax policy wonks to suggest that future benefits to workers will be paid only by high-income or corporate taxpayers in the form of cash taxes levied in the future. This is to suggest that high-income or corporate taxpayers will someday fund the tax base, so this assumption about who might pay taxes in the future should be "booked" today in the formulation of tax policy.[15] The method can be illustrated as follows:

	Current Taxes	Future Benefits	Future Taxes	Net Gain Loss
Worker	(45)	45	0	0
High income	(45)	?	(45)	(90)
Corporation	(9)	?	?	?

The source of federal revenue to fund future Social Security benefits is presumed to be federal income taxes from high-income persons, even though the federal government today receives most of its revenue from a combination of wage and income taxation. The assumption makes it possible to discuss transfer payments as relating to hypothetical taxes paid by the wealthy in a future period, even though transfer payments today are made by workers—and will likely always be made by workers. This method also simply ignores the fact that the federal government runs a deficit now and presumably will run a larger deficit at the time future transfer payments should be made. So, even if progressive tax rates meant that the wealthy were funding the tax base, indeed this would not mean that the wealthy were funding the federal budget, since the federal budget might be funded by borrowing from either past or future workers.

Deception #5. Statutory tax rates, not effective tax rates, are what's important to tax policy

Political debates on tax policy usually center on the level of statutory tax rates. For example, in the lead-up to the passage of the Tax Cuts and Jobs Act of 2017, most of the discourse was related to whether the 35 percent corporate tax rate was too high. None other than the Council on Foreign Relations even claimed that the US corporate tax rate was "one of the highest corporate tax rates in the world."[16] Nearly all news media outlets at the time discussed corporate taxation according to the premise that the taxes paid must be high because the statutory tax rate is high—what a farce!

The misleading aspect of this discourse has to do with the effective tax rate. In tax parlance, the term "effective tax rate" refers to the tax rate after all incentives or reductions are considered. In this case, a large corporation may receive incentives that reduce the effective tax rate from the statutory rate to some lesser amount, and *that* amount is the corporate tax rate. Of course, the effective tax rate is a function of many different tax deductions from the statutory rate or other incentives. Estimating the effective tax rate requires having knowledge of the amount of income and the amount of deductions and other incentives available to a taxpayer, such as a large corporation. Most of the time, neither of those variables is known by anyone inside or outside the corporation until the time that the corporate tax return is prepared after the close of the tax year. Therefore, it is entirely possible that a high statutory tax rate (e.g., 35 percent) could apply to the corporation *but* it has a low effective tax rate because of available tax incentives and other deductions. This was broadly true of the US corporate tax system even before the Tax Cuts and Jobs Act of 2017; the effective tax rate on US multinational firms was quite low, most scholars thought no higher than 21 percent.

My view was then that the 21 percent estimate is too high because it failed to reasonably consider the accumulation of a corporation's overseas profits. An effective tax rate is calculated as follows: Effective Tax Rate = Total Taxes / Total Income.[17] Both the taxes paid amount in the numerator and the income amount in the denominator must be accurate in order to calculate the effective tax rate. Increasing the amount of corporate profits would reduce the effective tax rate by increasing the denominator of the fraction or the amount of income which the corporation had earned without changing the amount of taxes it had paid. By more accurately stating the amount of corporate profits, I was previously able to estimate average effective tax rate in 2007 instead at 16 percent, as opposed to 21 percent as others had calculated, but in any case trending sharply downward.[18] The downward trend indicated that the average effective tax rate was declining by roughly 0.5 percent per year—so following this trend, as of 2016, the effective tax rate would have been closer to 11 percent. Of course, some large companies pay less than the average rate, especially companies in the pharmaceutical, high tech and automobile industries, where the effective tax rate may be between 0 percent and 5 percent in most years.[19]

Therefore, the US corporate tax rate was not properly described as *high*. The average effective tax rate for large corporations was somewhere between 10 percent and 21 percent at the time of the reforms. The effective corporate tax rate in the United States was actually relatively *low* in comparison to other countries. The relatively low rate was due to various factors, including specific incentives contained within the tax code itself. For example, prior to the corporate tax cuts, the US corporate tax system was structured to allow for three things: (1) broad deferral of large corporations' offshore earnings until profits were repatriated, if ever, (2) a lack of tax enforcement on intercompany transfer pricing (so firms were freely able to shift profits into tax havens or other favorable jurisdictions) and (3) no enforcement of the accumulated earnings tax for large multinational corporations. All of this meant that corporations were not required to pay dividends, which might have triggered additional tax at the shareholder level. Thus, the system was quite favorable for large corporations because it was unlikely that corporate earnings would be taxed much, if at all.

The pertinent question, then, is why would anyone talk about tax policy in terms of statutory tax rates rather than effective tax rates? Large corporations have smart tax advisors, so ought to be able to estimate the effective tax rate for their potential earnings. Those tax advisors would be aware that the statutory tax rate would not be the rate they would be required to pay on any future profits. Yet most of the discussion at the time was a superficial treatment of statutory tax rates; very little discourse reached an analysis of corporate effective tax rates.

For their part, economists have long recognized that the most important statistic for tax policy is likely the effective tax rate, not the statutory tax rate. The use of effective tax rates is extremely problematic for economic theorizing, however. Data on effective tax rates is not readily available to economists, and it would always be firm-specific anyway. Absent a solution, this makes it nearly impossible to say anything precise about tax policy by way of economic theory.

A solution was nonetheless identified within economic theory to render it relevant to tax policy notwithstanding an inability to know what effective tax rates actually are. Economists simply invented as a solution the "marginal tax rate," which is nearly always equivalent to the statutory tax rate. The "marginal tax rate" is a hypothetical rate that the firm would pay on an extra dollar of earnings above what the company is expected to earn. In economic theorizing, it is posited that firm-level decisions relate to the marginal tax rate, or the tax rate on "extra" or incremental earnings arising from new investments. The marginal tax rate is generally presumed by economists to be equal to the statutory tax rate. This means that in the formulation of tax policy economists generally posit that large corporations will make decisions based on the full statutory rate rather than the average effective tax rate. So, cutting tax rates for large corporations could therefore be seen as potentially beneficial even where the large corporation is not currently paying much (or any) taxes because corporations might be expected to take investment decisions under the countervailing premise that they would estimate taxes on earnings from that "extra" profit from investment and reduce the expected rate of return by the amount of "extra" taxes to be paid. In any case, economists are comfortable speaking about tax policy in terms of statutory tax rates rather than effective tax rates, because it is simply presumed as a matter of economic theory, without any evidence of course, that firms would expect to pay the statutory tax rate on any incremental earnings from new investment. That view is wrong most of the time because firms typically make decisions about business investments considering the average effective tax rate, not the marginal or statutory tax rate. In actual practice out in the real world, the CEOs of large corporations are infamous for signing the papers on major investment or M&A (Mergers and Acquisitions) decisions without consulting the tax department in advance. The typical example (often discussed by tax professionals with a chuckle or sigh) is the CEO who agrees to do a stock deal rather than an asset deal, and then finds out the next day when the stock deal is disclosed to the tax department, that the depreciation on assets held by the target company does not step up to the price paid on a stock deal but it does an asset deal. And, the difference can amount to many millions for a sizeable target company.

Deception #6. High business tax rates reduce economic growth by reducing the economic return on investment

The income tax is a voluntary tax in the sense that reinvesting profits into the business generally reduces the tax base (or the amount of taxable income) that is subject to tax. Simply put, any income tax is levied on the tax base, which is the amount of profit minus any deductions. Business deductions can be claimed by, for example, reinvesting in or expanding an existing business or business line. Consider a small dry-cleaning business that generates $100,000 of profit each year. If the owners open a new dry-cleaning store, then they can apply various deductions related to expenses and depreciation from the new store against the profits from the existing stores. These expenses might total $60,000, netted against the profit from the other stores, and so reduce the tax base from $100,000 to $40,000. Therefore, the business expansion automatically reduces the tax base from the existing profitable business lines. For this reason, rapidly expanding businesses often pay no income tax at all, even when they have high profits and positive cash flow. Therefore, the income tax on business can be understood as a voluntary tax. Other types of tax, especially earned income tax, are not voluntary in this way because those earnings generally may not be delayed or offset by other deductions.

The companies that are most concerned about income taxes are accordingly those that are not expanding by reinvesting their profits, especially large corporations given the tendency of large firms to operate without capital reinvestment. If a large corporation operates the business as an annuity, to generate economic rent from business lines without having to reinvest profits or expand, then income taxes are likely to apply on profits from existing business lines. In this case, the corporation has not taken advantage of the voluntary nature of the income tax system by reinvesting profits to reduce the tax base. One objective of tax policy in a capitalist society is to encourage capital reinvestment to foster economic growth, and if this does not happen for some reason then capitalism gets sick and does not function as well as it should. Hence, where a company operates its business as an annuity and does not have any capital reinvestment plans, then that company is not as likely to facilitate economic growth. A tax policy expert might say it's a good time for the company to pay some tax, since there are apparently no plans to expand the business by capital reinvestment. Hence, the remittance of corporate tax by a company that operates its business as an annuity, without plans for capital reinvestment, does not seem harmful to economic growth, because the capital converted into tax was not going to be reinvested anyway.

This lesson regarding the voluntary nature of the tax system can be applied even more broadly to international tax policy. Imagine a multinational corporation that is profitable in many different jurisdictions. The company needs to make some capital reinvestment in the form of research and development or similar capital expenditures. These investments will result in an income tax deduction currently (or going forward into the future in the form of depreciation and amortization), but only in the jurisdiction where the capital is deployed. The company can choose in which jurisdiction it will make these capital reinvestments. So, in which jurisdiction will the company reinvest—a low-tax jurisdiction or a high-tax jurisdiction?

Economic theory says that the company will select a low-tax jurisdiction because any profits arising from the investment will be subject to less tax. However, any tax lawyer or accountant worth their salt would select the high-tax jurisdiction. This is because the investment gives rise to tax deductions immediately, and those deductions have value right away. Tax deductions are also worth more in the higher-tax jurisdiction to the extent that they offset profit in the high-tax jurisdiction; in other words, by reducing taxable income in the jurisdiction with the higher tax rate, the gross amount of taxable income is reduced by more than claiming those tax deductions in, say, a tax haven where the value of tax deductions is $0 (e.g., a 0 percent tax rate). The time value of money further requires that deductions taken today are worth more than deductions tomorrow. Furthermore, because large corporations usually can shift income by transfer-pricing techniques into low-tax jurisdictions, corporate tax planners simply presume the ability to shift income and thereby not pay tax at high rates.[20]

This technical explanation explains why nearly all capital investment flows into countries with relatively high corporate tax rates, such as Germany, South Korea, Japan, and (previously) the United States. Large corporations nearly always invest into high-tax jurisdictions, contrary to the predictions of economic theory. Corporate tax cuts paradoxically have the effect of reducing the attractiveness of that country for capital *reinvestment*. A multinational company seeking to maximize the value of present tax deductions would instead choose to reinvest capital into the higher-tax jurisdiction. But this is true only where the multinational firm is already profitable in the higher-tax jurisdiction, but this will nearly always be the case and should be presumed in the design of tax policy.

Another widely held belief about taxes and tax policy is that corporations are subject to two layers of taxation—once at the firm level, and again at the shareholder level—often referred to as *double taxation*. Tax commentators often refer to the double taxation of corporate profits as harmful to economic growth and as a justification for reducing the corporate rate. This is nonsense. The second layer of shareholder-level tax never has a chance to arise if the corporation continues to grow and reinvest profits into existing business lines, and accordingly, does not elect to pay dividends. As a general matter, large corporations are not forced to pay shareholder dividends because the Internal Revenue Service does not enforce the accumulated earnings tax under IRC §531 et seq. against those corporations, so any shareholder-level tax is simply delayed indefinitely until the corporation chooses to pay dividends, or never. Also, even if dividends are paid by the corporation to shareholders, not all shareholders are taxable on dividends received, such as when shares are held by a pension or sovereign investment fund, in a retirement plan such as a 401(k), or by any other nontaxable shareholder. Tax advisors to large corporations generally do not expect to pay a higher rate of corporate tax irrespective of the corporate statutory tax rate, which is why they choose to operate in corporate form in the first place. The availability of corporate-level tax deductions, lack of tax enforcement by the Internal Revenue Service especially in respect to transfer pricing by multinational firms, and the potential to delay the levy of tax at the shareholder level by not paying dividends represent several reasons why the corporate form is selected by tax experts for the operation of large business irrespective of the corporate statutory tax rate.

Deception #7. The working poor don't pay taxes because income tax rates are progressive

The tax system that applies to the wealthy and large corporations differs significantly from that which applies to workers who are paid wages and are immediately subject to taxes on that labor income. This is because nearly all earned income is currently subject to tax. Earned income is also generally not offset or reduced by deductions. Any earned income is taxed immediately on the full amount without any reduction. In contrast, the wealthy and large corporations are usually able to delay (or "defer") tax or not pay tax on the full amount of profits. Earned income is therefore always part of the tax base and almost never reduced by deductions. The progressive rate structure of the income tax does not offset these disadvantages. Labor income may always be disadvantaged under that system of automatic deferral of taxation for capital income but not labor income irrespective of any progressivity in the tax rates if there is the possibility of deferral to capital. For example, if the statutory tax rate on capital were set at 99 percent, and the tax rate on labor at only 10 percent, if deferral was still available to capital, the tax system might still favor capital despite the significant difference in the statutory tax rates. It simply is not possible to coherently discuss tax policy solely in terms of statutory tax rates without knowledge of the availability of deferral to capital under the tax laws.

Taxes are levied on earned income relatively simply: by multiplying the tax rate times the tax base. And, the tax rate on earned income is high. In addition to that high tax rate, the Social Security taxes levied in the United States are not progressively indexed.[21] For labor income, a worker may often pay federal income taxes of up to 38 percent, plus state and local income taxes, often 6 percent, plus Social Security and Medicare taxes. That's roughly 60 percent. And then, once the worker pays the 60 percent in taxes on earned income, lots of other taxes are also required to be paid, like sales taxes (often 6 percent on purchases), property taxes, (typically 3–5 percent of average earnings), gasoline tax (typically 2 percent or more of average earnings), a host of government fees (ranging from 2 percent to 5 percent of average earnings), and on and on. If all these taxes are added up, then nearly everything the worker earns is transferred back to the government in one form or another. If a worker has something left over after paying all these taxes, it should really be considered something of a miracle. One of the most significant deceptions in tax policy is encouraging workers to think that the wealthy and large corporations also pay confiscatory rates of tax similar to how workers pay taxes on their earned income. A second deception is to encourage workers to think that some progressivity in the income tax rates means that they are not paying a rate equal to that of a higher-income person; that is simply false. Wealthy people are wealthy in part because they tend to hold assets that have seen great increases in value, but they are not taxed on those increases as if they were income earned by and through work.

Deception #8. There are no social costs to high taxes on workers

The economic theory of taxation might sound complicated, but it's simple, really. Economic theory posits that only high-income workers and firms will choose to produce less economic output if they are taxed. This posited reduction in economic output is referred to as the *deadweight loss* of income taxation.[22] The deadweight loss from taxation is a subtraction to economic activity and to tax collections from the taxation of the wealthy only—there is no corresponding deadweight loss from the taxation of working people posited in economic theory. Thus, although evidence for the deadweight loss is lacking, it is posited to accrue only for the wealthy, not for lower-income workers. The assumption is that no matter how much tax workers are required to pay, there is no reduction in economic output from those taxes on workers. In other words, as far as economics is concerned there are no social costs to high taxes on workers. Workers simply don't count in economic theory—exactly as Thomas Malthus said long ago.

Economics has not changed much since Malthus's time. We have today really a formal way of applying Malthusian theory through the tax system. A significant problem in the present day is the lack of data to support these economic ideas. Scientists often call data *evidence*. To see if something is true, scientists like to look at data or evidence. For nearly all economic conclusions about tax policy, the data suggest the opposite result from the one proposed by economic theory. What does that mean? Often those economic conclusions are not supported by empirical evidence, and are sometimes just plain wrong.

It turns out that taxing workers at high rates creates a negative social cost. There should be a subtraction to economic output in economic theory representing a deadweight loss from labor taxation, but there isn't. These social costs from worker taxation relate to various areas including

- Public health—Workers seem to get sick more often and require costly health care under high-wage tax regimes. The negative economic result occurs because costs of health care are quite high because another person or governmental entity must pay for the incremental health care costs resulting from taxing labor at high rates that might be avoided simply by reducing the tax rates on workers.
- Child outcomes—Workers often have children, and high taxes on workers means they have less to invest in their children. A system designed to tax parents is an expensive design because society must try to remediate any deficits that occur amidst the chaos and uncertainty of parenting on a shoestring budget.
- Reduced or eliminated small business activity—The high tax rates on workers apply also to small businesses, including most types of entrepreneurial activity. Since the tax rates are exceptionally high on small business activity, this is detrimental to the formation of small business and tends to favor large corporations in the marketplace where small business operates in competition with large corporations.

It is very important to note that the point of this book is *not* that high tax rates on workers are unfair. Rather, the key observation of this book is that high rates of wage taxes are expensive (or inefficient) because taxing workers creates social costs that may even exceed the amount of tax collected.

Deception #9. Workers and poor people are cognitively inferior to the wealthy and unable to make rational economic decisions

The idea of the cognitive inferiority of the poor arose in the subfield of economics referred to as *behavioral economics*. Although behavioral economists don't say explicitly that the poor are not as intelligent as the wealthy, their analysis is always premised on that assumption. Rich people are presumed to be smart and able to make rational decisions in the manner economists expect. Of course, the first decision that all presumptively rational and wealthy people make is that they should pay $0 in taxes and that workers should pay all the taxes. The further implication is that the wealthy should make all economic decisions since they are able to think rationally. Notably, this was exactly Thomas Malthus's view, so today's economic theory has reverted to an overtly Malthusian ideal.

I wish to challenge here the views both that workers are not rational and that the wealthy are rational or at least more often rational than the poor in decision making. To do so, I need to first disprove the claim that workers or the poor are irrational under the framework of behavioral economics. That's easy.

To my knowledge, there is no empirical data whatsoever about consumer preferences as applied in the field of behavioral economics related to taxation or tax policy that would allow for the creation of a welfare function. The absence of data means in the context of taxing sugar-sweetened beverages, for example, that it may be true that poor people make a bad decision in drinking sugar beverages, the badness of that decision to consume sugar in economic terms is always relative to cost. Economists call this relativity of cost to choice the *welfare function*. All economics depends on these welfare functions—they account for much of the field of economics. The basic assertion in behavioral economics is that the poor person spends \$0.50 on a sugar beverage and gets back 2 utiles, or some other amount, of welfare. The number of utiles is arbitrary. We only know for sure that it would be irrational for a wealthy person to consume a sugar beverage. We know absolutely nothing about whether it is "rational" (as economists often say) for a poor person to whom price is important to consume a sugar beverage given the respective cost of \$0.50. For the wealthy person, the \$0.50 is not a material amount of money. A wealthy person could get the same 2 utiles of welfare by choosing a non-sugar-sweetened beverage that costs \$4. The difference in price between the \$4 and the \$0.50 ought to mean nothing to the wealthy person in economic terms. But the difference in price does potentially mean something to the poor person, who might be forced to choose between the \$4 beverage and some other consumer item that costs \$4 and which also yields welfare of an equivalent amount. To a poorer person, perhaps earning minimum wage, \$4 is a lot of money and reflects roughly the value of an hour's work after tax withholding. Our economist friends have simply never studied the significance of that difference in price relative to cost, so it's all conjecture. In fact, there is no welfare function, or even any attempt to create a welfare function, for either the wealthy person or the poor person within behavioral economics. All we have in behavioral economics reflects the prejudices of the economists telling us their conclusions without any attempt to provide data. Behavioral economics is essentially economists looking in the mirror and not liking what they see very much.

Second, the wealthy do not seem to act rationally, at least much of the time. The wealthy eat foie gras, collect private jets, build private yachts at ruinous expense, travel by dangerous helicopters, acquire multiple mansions and houses—none of this is rational economic behavior that works toward increasing aggregate wealth. The spending of vast fortunes on personal comforts does not maximize individual utility; personal comforts exist on a broad U-shaped function where some is good and too much begins to yield declining rates of return or even to decrease overall utility. Furthermore, some happiness appears to involve participating in projects with others, or helping other people. As the wealthy are now able to avoid most forms of taxation, and increasingly build walls and retreat into private castles, it seems possible that the government might set out to increase aggregate utility by mandating the idle (and, arguably *irrational*) wealthy classes to participate in society by helping others and thereby to increase the utility and well-being of the wealthy by mandating some type of public service. Utility gains could accrue to the wealthy by participation in society even if the wealthy did not actually do anything helpful for the rest of us. Alternately, if significant taxes were someday levied on the wealthy classes, the wealthy might even be expected to gain utility if the benefits of social programs derived from tax revenue were earmarked and reported back to individual taxpayers, such that each person could be given examples of what their tax revenue actually purchased (i.e., your tax remittance paid for 20 children to receive Head Start education, or your tax remittance purchased one F-22 fighter jet, and so on).

Deception #10. Tax cuts for large corporations are the only viable tax policy option and never tax cuts for small business

The design of the tax system also requires at times selective amnesia. For example, everyone seems to agree that small businesses are the engine of economic growth in capitalism. So, why do OECD (Organization for Economic Cooperation and Development) nations so often choose to tax small businesses at rates of roughly 60 percent and more but large corporations at effective rates often 10 percent or less? It seems that in the course of setting tax policy economists and politicians seem to suddenly forget something that has already been determined by everyone concerned and essentially agreed to be true: that small businesses are the engine of economic growth. If small businesses cause economic growth, and lower taxes are helpful to small businesses, then no tax policy expert should ever talk about anything other than cutting taxes for small business.

In addition, policymakers seem to show selective amnesia about many other important matters of tax policy analysis, such as the value of tax deferral to the owners of capital. After the Tax Cuts and Jobs Act of 2017, which reduced the statutory corporate tax rate from 35 percent to 21 percent, one tax organization was still calling for further tax cuts for large corporations on the ridiculous premise that the US corporate tax system was not "competitive" based on a comparison of statutory tax rates, alone.[23] The approach is to switch the policy discourse to inquiry regarding whether the statutory tax rate for large corporations as just too high or too low. That's another way of saying that the topic of conversation simply switches back to the normative idea that large corporations should not pay taxes. But, large corporations pay tax at the effective tax rate, not the statutory tax rate; and, the availability of tax deferral to the wealthy and large corporations is more important than the statutory tax rate.

Deception #11. *Tax cuts for large corporations will reduce prices on consumer products*

Many economists have proposed that corporate tax cuts result in lower consumer prices. Yet, this simply isn't true and represents probably the most obvious attempt at outright deception of all the deceptions discussed thus far in this book. The taxing authority in the United Kingdom even published a white paper along these lines suggesting that there are "dynamic effects" of corporate tax cuts with all sorts of potential benefits that ripple through the economy, although the benefits are never and have never been observed in all prior instances of corporate tax cuts.[24] In nearly every field of human inquiry apart from economic theory, scholars at least try to use evidence to determine whether a policy claim should be accepted as true. The question then arises: What is the evidence that corporate tax cuts cause price reductions on consumer products?

If you were conscious in the latter part of 2017 and early 2018, then you might be able to answer that question based on experience. In November 2017, the Tax Cuts and Jobs Act of 2017 was negotiated and passed by Congress and sent to the president for signature. The act involved one of the most significant corporate tax cuts in the history of the United States, reducing the rate from 35 percent to 21 percent. In addition, the system of international taxation was changed such that large corporations no longer had to try so hard to avoid paying tax on overseas profits. Partly because of the reduction in statutory tax rates, the actual amounts of corporate tax remitted by large corporations were significantly reduced. Although no one knows for sure by *how* much, the Congressional Budget Office initially estimated that the reduction would cost $1.456 trillion. I suspect the amount of taxes payable will be reduced by more than half; that is, on average, I expect that companies that were paying some amount of tax are now paying less than half of what they were paying. And, those tax benefits were booked by the large corporations immediately under the applicable accounting rules. Many corporate executives got huge bonuses for doing such a good job in boosting corporate profits by paying less corporate tax.

But, did the prices of consumer products decrease after the corporate tax cuts as economists predicted? Obviously not. Not even a little bit. The fact is that consumer prices continued to increase after the massive corporate tax cuts. In other words, prices failed to decline even after one of the largest corporate tax cuts in human history. Simply put, corporate taxes dropped by roughly half, but the price of a new car did not drop from $35,000 to $17,500, or even to $34,000. In nearly all cases the prices of consumer products did not decline to any measureable degree and even went up. So, we might ask: What does that say about economic theory on taxes and tax policy?

As will be explained in the next chapter, economic theory regarding taxes is not premised on evidence or data. So, no economist has ever gone back to the drawing board because his or her predictions on tax policy did not turn out to be true. Economic ideas about taxes are almost never revised when better evidence or data becomes available. This is because corporate tax theory is a justification along the lines of moral philosophy; it is not a causal theory. But it is also true that no economist ever said that corporate tax cuts should be expected to cause price reductions. The formalization of some causal hypothesis in advance of testing by observation would be considered necessary in any field of actual science apart from economics as applied to tax policy. The lack of any causal theory in economics means there is no true "science"—and accordingly, no testing of predictions made by economists—about corporate tax cuts or other matters of tax policy. Rather, tax policy is all a magic show put on to trick you.

So, how does this magic trick on corporate tax cuts and consumer prices work? Why do corporate tax cuts not lead to lower consumer prices? Well, perhaps for lots of reasons, but I suspect the most important one is that large corporations set the price for their products based on what the customer is willing and able to pay, not by an anticipated level of after-tax profits. Prices and profits are not the same thing. Profits are not fixed such that a corporate tax cut means that the price for the product can and should be reduced. This is also to say that the universe economists live in is not the same universe we consumers live in. In fact, if a corporate executive set prices in the manner that economists propose, he or she would probably be fired. Corporations are tasked with maximizing profit, not with maximizing fairness to consumers in the relative prices of products. Furthermore, the markets in which large corporations operate are not efficient. Many large corporations compete in markets where small businesses have been bankrupted over the past decade or so by both the tax system and trade policy, so there is little or no price competition for the large corporations. The simple fact is that consumer prices did not noticeably decrease after the passage of the Tax Cuts and Jobs Act of 2017. Accordingly, it is not necessary to debate back and forth why this is so or might be so. We have strong and essentially incontrovertible evidence now that corporate tax cuts do not lower consumer prices. Furthermore, it would be a relatively easy task for economists to gather evidence about consumer prices in relation to corporate tax cuts and put their theories to the test. Since this has not been done (and will likely never be done unless some objection is raised) it is appropriate to now begin to reject the predictions of economic theory on the imaginary pass-through of corporate tax reductions to consumers in the form of price reductions, at least until some empirical evidence is collected on consumer prices and correlative tests performed on these supposed dynamic effects of corporate tax cuts.

THE TAXATION OF WORKERS

Justifications for why workers should always pay the taxes in society are easily found in libertarian, economic or liberal writings on tax and the supposed philosophy thereof. However, the conclusions of these philosophical writings are essentially all the same: it is right, good, fair, efficient or essential that workers pay all the taxes. Indeed, the conclusions are all so much the same that tax scholars no longer even attempt to distinguish the various types of philosophy relevant to taxation. No matter what you read, it will contain justifications for tax policy that are always premised on taxing workers.

In the first, place, by the actual numbers, it is unrealistic to expect that workers could really pay any more in taxes than they already do. Although the respective terminology has not been widely adopted in the United States, in Europe tax scholars would say that workers lack the "ability to pay" any more in taxes than they already do because they lack the disposable funds to pay incremental taxes. Further taxes on workers would entail larger portions of American society becoming insolvent even while working multiple jobs. The taxation of workers has essentially been maximized to allow for the wealthy to accumulate the largest possible hordes of capital. Yet, the prior tax literature does *not* say, that tax policy is a trick designed to allow for the accumulations of capital that is premised on an illusion of progressivity, fairness and efficiency. These concepts actually have been created as a means to keep the workers paying unreasonable amounts of tax into the system. The truth is, the tax system is regressive, unfair and inefficient. One objective of this book is to attempt to shift tax discourse from discussions primarily among the wealthy about how to best justify an oppressive, inefficient and unfair tax system to various realistic discussions about how to improve the system for the benefit of the working people that comprise a democratic society.

Existing tax policy literature is aimed at the wealthy—both individuals and corporations—and its purpose is to justify their accumulation of huge fortunes. This is to justify the concentration of wealth rather than a diffusion of wealth that is achieved primarily through the tax system. Some wealthy persons do feel guilty about not paying much in taxes while workers do. And moreover, the wealthy are able to complain loudly about tax policy to policymakers in government and the news media. Furthermore, many outspoken moral philosophers and economists claim to be experts in tax policy, but they often have little or no training in taxation and thus no idea about how the tax system works in actual practice. This combination of vociferous complaining by the wealthy about taxation and lay commentary on tax policy makes it possible for regular people who are trying to understand the tax system to believe that the wealthy pay taxes when they actually do not.

The recent tax cuts targeted for large corporations have not been matched to any spending cuts, so tax policy wonks say they are not "revenue neutral." Notably, the Tax Reform Act of 1986 was at least ostensibly revenue neutral, so it was not funded by increased deficits. The recent tax cuts are instead funded by increased government debt today, along with targeted tax increases on the middle class and tax increases on the working class, to be collected at some point either now or in the future. Therefore, the term "tax cuts" is not the right term to describe this state of affairs of tax cuts for large corporations funded by increased deficits; instead, this latter push toward increased deficits should be referred to as *tax increases for workers either now or in the future*. Sometime since the Reagan administration, the actual meaning of the words *tax cuts* has shifted so as to not include any offsets or future taxes necessary to repay additional debt incurred today. Future workers will be asked to pay interest and principal on the government debt taken on to fund today's tax cuts for large corporations. The actual meaning of the words *tax cuts* has thereby been altered in the political discourse. The result is an Orwellian version of tax policy such that words no longer mean what they used to mean, even to politicians of the same political party.

As to the second element of postmodernism in tax policy—that the wealthy view workers as the "little people"— it may seem hard to believe that the wealthy hold such a view. Yet, famous economic scholars assert that the poor are generally unable to make rational economic decisions by their own terms.[25] This is essentially Thomas Malthus's view brought back to life and into the mainstream. Tax research by scholars all over the world—from

England, to Singapore, to Austria and to the United States—have proceeded enthusiastically to argue for new regressive types of Pigouvian taxes to be levied on the working class. Here, Pigouvian taxes refer to taxes levied on specific goods and products with externalities thought to be harmful to the people that consume the product. Scholars are seemingly coming out of the woodwork, even from nontax disciplines, to argue in favor of special taxes on any product that is used predominantly by the poor and also thought to be harmful. The levy of these taxes is intended always to correct the irrational behavior of the poor as a class—but never the wealthy! Of course, no economist has ever discussed the irrational behavior of the wealthy and proposed addressing it through the tax system. Rather, the economic analysis is always presupposed on levying taxes on the poor and also on workers.

An overwhelming problem with this methodology is that workers cannot and should not be lumped into a class with the poor. The only reason to do so is that the wealthy view the world in this weird way where the categories of *working* and *poor* are understood as synonymous. The wealthy often view nonworkers (existing on government transfer payments, for example) as essentially the same as persons working but not earning much due to low wages. For their part, the blue-collar workers of America have no idea that the wealthy draw this false equivalency and view them in the same category as nonworkers. Furthermore, no economist has ever acknowledged the problem that the workers already pay the maximum amount of taxes they could possibly be expected to pay, via all sorts of different categories of taxation: wage withholding, income tax, sales tax, property tax, gasoline tax and a host of government fees. As such, it is practically impossible for additional taxes to be levied on workers without canceling out a supposed efficiency gain from new Pigouvian tax types that economists say arises from some other regressive tax already in force. In other words, Pigouvian taxes that cancel out other Pigouvian taxes cannot yield an efficiency gain because workers do not have an unlimited pool of funds from which to pay all of these taxes. In fact, there are limits on the taxes that workers can ultimately pay whether economists set out to identify those limits or not.

NOTES

1 *See* Arthur Villasanta, *Jeff Bezos' DC Mansion Has 25 Bathrooms and Reddit Was Not Having It*, International Business Times (Nov. 7, 2019), https://www.ibtimes.com/jeff-bezos-dc-mansion-has-25-bathrooms-reddit-was-not-having-it-2861437. Accessed Nov. 10, 2019.

2 Tax Cuts and Jobs Act of 2017, Pub. L. No. 115–97. References to data on federal tax revenues and the corporate share of the tax base are from the U.S. Treasury Department data (Fiscal Year 2017) and Congressional Budget Office (CBO)

estimates; CBO, *Options for Reducing the Deficit* (Dec. 2016), https://www.cbo.gov/publication/52142. Accessed Nov. 10, 2019.

3 Tax Cuts and Jobs Act of 2017, Pub. L. No. 115–97. References to data on federal tax revenues and the corporate share of the tax base are from the U.S. Treasury Department data (Fiscal Year 2017) and Congressional Budget Office (CBO) estimates; CBO, *Options for Reducing the Deficit* (Dec. 2016), https://www.cbo.gov/publication/52142. Accessed Nov. 10, 2019.

Federal income tax revenues derived from labor in comparison to business or investment, see: Jay Soled & Kathleen DeLaney Thomas, *Automation and the Income Tax*, 10:1 COLUMBIA J. OF TAX LAW, 1, 7–17 (2019).

4 Richard Hammer, *The Helmsleys: The Rise and Fall of Harry & Leona* (New York: NAL Books, 1990).

5 Matt Egan, *Just 4% of Companies Boosted Hiring Because of Tax Cuts*, CNN Business (Jan. 29, 2019) https://www.cnn.com/2019/01/28/business/tax-cuts-jobs-business-spending-nabe/index.html. Accessed Nov. 10, 2019 ("The expensive 2017 tax law failed to encourage Corporate America to embark on a boom in hiring or job-creating investment. Just 4% of business economists say their companies accelerated hiring because of the tax overhaul, according to a survey released Monday by the National Association for Business Economics."). And only 10% of business economists said their firms stepped up investments like building factories, buying equipment and purchasing software because of the tax law.

6 Data are available on the relation between tax base and GDP per capita. See Organization for Economic Cooperation and Development (OECD), http://www.oecd.org/tax/revenue-statistics-2522770x.htm; World Bank Data on GDP Levels Per Capita https://data.worldbank.org/indicator/NY.GDP.PCAP.CD?view=chart. I have previously compiled and published charts to illustrate the lack of any correlation between tax cuts and GDP per capita. See, e.g., Bret N. Bogenschneider, *Causation, Science & Taxation*, 10:1 ELON L. REV. 1 (2017); Bret N. Bogenschneider, *The Tax Paradox of Capital Investment*, 33:1 J. TAXATION OF INV. 59, 79 (2015).

7 Bret Bogenschneider & Ruth Heilmeier, *Income Elasticity and Inequality*, 5:1 INT. J. ECON. & BUS. LAW 34 (2016).

8 Switzerland has a federal tax, a cantonal tax and some municipal taxes, which when combined are relatively low. For an explanation and tax rates on the individual tax system in Swiss localities, see Federal Government of Switzerland, *The Swiss Tax System* (Dec. 2018), https://www.efd.admin.ch/efd/en/home/themen/steuern/steuern-national/the-swiss-tax-system/fb-schweizer-steuersystem.html. Accessed Nov. 10, 2019.

9 An interesting illustration is the deceased multimillionaire, Jeffrey Epstein, who was once a scion of the investment banking scene. See generally, Greg Norman, *Jeffrey Epstein's Private Caribbean Island Had Mysterious Safe, Former Employee Claims*, Fox News (July 12, 2019), https://www.foxnews.com/us/jeffrey-epstein-caribbean-island-mystery. Accessed Nov. 10, 2019. Obviously, Epstein's capital investments into his various sex palaces in the Caribbean and New York City were not efficient investments for broader society.

10 St. Louis Federal Reserve, *Why Are Corporations Holding So Much Cash?* (Jan. 1, 2013), https://www.stlouisfed.org/publications/regional-economist/january-2013/why-are-corporations-holding-so-much-cash. Accessed Nov. 10, 2019.

11 See Jeffry Bartash, *Repatriated Profits Total $465 Billion After Trump Tax Cuts, Leaving $2.5 Trillion Overseas*, MarketWatch (Sept. 19, 2018), http://www.marketwatch.com/story/repatriated-profits-total-nearly-500-billion-after-trump-tax-cuts-2018-09-19. Accessed Nov. 10, 2019.

12 For a general discussion of this idea, see: Benjamin Willis, *Fool Me Twice: Trump's Payroll Tax Cuts*, Tax Notes (Aug. 22, 2019) ("On August 20 President Trump said regarding tax cuts that the 'payroll tax is something that we think about, and a lot of people would like to see that, and that very much affects the workers of our country.' Such a strategy is based on the economic belief that reducing taxes on low- and middle-income Americans is the best way to ensure that consumers continue spending money and the economy is stimulated."), https://www.taxnotes.com/opinions/fool-me-twice-trumps-payroll-tax-cuts/2019/08/22/29vv7. Accessed Nov. 10, 2019.

13 Robert Frank, *Top 1% Pay Nearly Half of Federal Income Taxes*, CNBC (Apr. 14, 2015), https://www.cnbc.com/2015/04/13/top-1-pay-nearly-half-of-federal-income-taxes.html, citing Tax Policy Center, https://www.taxpolicycenter.org/research-commentary. Accessed Nov. 10, 2019

14 See, e.g., Stephen Moore, *Do the Rich Pay Their Fair Share?*, Heritage Foundation (Mar. 3, 2015), https://www.heritage.org/budget-and-spending/commentary/do-the-rich-pay-their-fair-share. Accessed Nov. 10, 2019 ("Suppose there were a banquet for 100 people and at the end of the night it was time to split the bill of $50 per person. If that bill were paid for the way we pay our income taxes, here is how it would work. Those in the top half of income would pay roughly $97 each and those in the bottom half of the income would pay an average of $3 each. Almost 40 people would pay nothing."); Adam Michel, *The New York Times Is Wrong. The Rich Pay More Taxes Than You Do*. The Heritage Foundation (Oct. 15, 2019), https://www.heritage.org/taxes/commentary/the-new-york-times-wrong-the-rich-pay-more-taxes-you-do. Accessed Nov. 10, 2019.

15 For an illustration of this method in the news media, see Michael R. Strain, *The Rich Really Do Pay Higher Taxes Than You*, Bloomberg Opinion (Oct. 10, 2019), https://www.bloombergquint.com/gadfly/the-rich-really-do-pay-higher-taxes-than-you ("This is half the story. When assessing the progressivity of the U.S. Federal system, it makes sense to look at both taxes and the means-tested transfer payments—Medicaid, Food stamps and Supplemental Security Income—that those taxes fund. *If you subtract these payments from federal taxes paid*.") (emphasis added).

16 See Council on Foreign Relations, *U.S. Corporate Tax Reform* (Nov. 3, 2017), https://www.cfr.org/backgrounder/us-corporate-tax-reform. Accessed Nov. 10, 2019.

17 See Brian Spilker et al. Taxation of Individuals and Business Entities (New York: McGraw Hill, 2020), at 1–9.

18 *See* Bret Bogenschneider, *The Effective Tax Rates of U.S. Firms with Permanent Deferral*, 145 TAX NOTES 1391 (2015).

19 Megan Cerullo, *60 of America's Biggest Companies Paid No Federal Income Tax in 2018*, CBS News (Apr. 12, 2019), https://www.cbsnews.com/news/2018-taxes-some-of-americas-biggest-companies-paid-little-to-no-federal-income-tax-last-year/. Accessed Nov. 10, 2019.

20 See Kimberly A. Clausing, *In Search of Corporate Tax Incidence*, 65 TAX L. REV. 433, 438–45 (2012).

21 See Sean Williams, *The Rich Are Costing Social Security Almost $150 Billion a Year*, The Motley Fool (Feb. 14, 2009), https://www.fool.com/retirement/2019/02/14/the-rich-are-costing-social-security-almost-150-bi.aspx. Accessed Nov. 10, 2019.

22 Martin Feldstein, *Tax Avoidance and the Deadweight Loss of the Income Tax*, 81:4 Rev. Econ. & Stat. 674 (1999).

23 Laura Davison, *U.S. Corporate Tax Code Still Ranks Below Average, Study Finds*, Bloomberg Tax (Oct.3, 2019), https://news.bloombergtax.com/daily-tax-report/u-s-corporate-tax-code-still-ranks-below-average-study-finds. Accessed Nov. 10, 2019, citing Statements of Daniel Bunn, Tax Foundation Director of Global Projects ("The U.S. is slightly more competitive partially because we have moved slightly toward a territorial system, but the rules that we use to tax profits overseas are still kind of middle-of-the-road if not lower half of the distribution").

24 HM Revenue & Customs, *Analysis of the Dynamic Effects of Corporation Tax Reductions* 19–30 (Dec. 5, 2013), http://www.gov.uk/government/uploads/system/uploads/attachment_data/file/263560/4069_CT_Dynamic_effects_paper_20130312_IW_v2.pdf. Accessed Nov. 10, 2019.

25 Richard Thaler & Cass Sunstein, *Libertarian Paternalism*, 93 American Econ. Rev. 175 (2003).

CHAPTER 1

TAX POLICY IN THE OVAL OFFICE

Chapter Summary: *The tax system as portrayed on television and in political discourse bears little resemblance to reality. Workers suffer from extremely high effective tax rates. Withholding out of workers' paychecks accounts for the vast majority of federal tax receipts— not less than 82 percent of the federal tax base. Even supposedly "bipartisan" tax statistics given by tax policy organizations are misleading, often reflecting the ideological beliefs of both political parties that workers should remit the bulk of the tax base. Because few economists have practical tax experience, they use these misleading and inaccurate statistics to create tax policy recommendations for the president. The quintessential example of politicized thinking on tax policy is the famous Laffer curve, which was later found to be utterly false. The Laffer curve predicted that tax receipts could be increased by cutting tax rates. In actuality, sustained economic growth can best be achieved by cutting taxes on workers and small businesses. Since economists follow a false narrative that economic growth will result from shifting the tax base toward workers, this essentially boxes the president into a corner, with little or no viable means to foster economic growth.*

In the first days or weeks in office, every president receives an initial briefing on the economic and tax policy from the chief economic advisor—the person whom the president has selected and put forward as his or her foremost economic and tax policy expert. This person is typically a well-known economist who may have some background in taxation, but often not. A deputy economic advisor who specializes in tax policy might also be involved. The deputy may have direct experience in government, usually with the Treasury Department or Internal Revenue Service, and has very specific knowledge about tax statistics and rates. The deputy is therefore a helpful associate, as he or she might respond to any specific questions the president has on tax rates or other policy matters. However, since nearly every economist in the world thinks he or she is an expert on all matters of taxation, this overconfidence means that is also entirely possible that the president's initial briefing could occur with no advisor present in the room who has any real or practical experience in taxation. This chapter addresses the role of the president in the first analysis of tax policy. Chapter 3 addresses the role of Congress in tax policy formation, including the significance of "scoring" tax legislation by the Congressional Budget Office.

The lack of practical experience in taxation among economic advisors is important because there is almost no data on anything related to taxation. Hence, in the formation of tax policy there is generally not empirical evidence related to how a change in policy might create a specific policy outcome. Therefore everything in taxation is speculative at least to some degree. Tax policy largely comprises guesswork about the potential causal relations between variables. The most famous guess by an economist on tax policy matters is Laffer's drawing of a curve on a restaurant napkin. Laffer posited an imaginary world of a U-shaped tax function. He proposed that society is on the downward-sloping side, so where tax rates are reduced, then tax receipts might go up.[1] Let me say that again: Laffer thought that by reducing the tax rate, the government would collect more tax. This laughable idea was advanced during the Reagan administration and was used to justify and formulate tax policy at the time. Empirical testing later showed that the guess was completely wrong, even though many economists of the day thought it was plausible. I mention the Laffer curve here in the introduction because it occurred in relatively recent history, and the economic models that gave rise to this infamous guess have not changed much since that time and even through the present day. So, an economist could still make that same guess today and not be laughed out of the room. This is truly odd. One lesson from experience with the Laffer curve debacle is that, for the most part, economists do not abandon theories of tax policy even when they are proven utterly and completely wrong.

To explain how this could be, and to explain how tax policy is formulated in the absence of any data or evidence, a brief mention of how economics functions as a discipline is necessary. In economics, tax policy analysis nearly always begins with the following premise: "Imagine a world where X, Y, and Z." The imaginary world is then described in the form of equations with a series of Greek letters. The economic "experts" in tax policy rely on deductive analysis of the Greek letters to derive what they believe is sensible tax policy for the imaginary world they have posited. As an example, with the Laffer curve, the proposal of the U-shaped tax function might be true somewhere in the universe—just not on Earth. So, where the imaginary world does not match the actual world, the analysis is useless. Turns out, the Laffer curve is useless for this exact reason—it's imaginary—all evidence suggests the tax remittance function isn't U-shaped. Even if it were, we definitely aren't on the downward-sloping side of the U-shaped function that Laffer imagined. The famous philosopher

Karl Popper spent a lot of time explaining how to refute nonexistential (or, nonexisting) ideas like the Laffer curve in fields other than taxation, and his thought led to a shift toward knowledge premised on science rather than superstition. Science itself requires that the imaginations of scientists in any field ultimately be checked to see if they correspond to the actual world before people believe in the imagination to a more significant degree.[2]

In comparison, tax practitioners—meaning persons with experience in the tax system—generally do not use this economic approach to causal knowledge about taxation and tax policy. Tax practitioners typically begin with the premise: "I remember a situation where X, Y, and Z." Even though a process of remembering is not a valid method of testing causal beliefs, it is a valid, and valuable, method of proposing a possible theory of causation. This difference in the process of forming ideas about causation between economic modeling and tax practitioner memory is significant. The tax practitioner possesses what is essentially clinical knowledge of taxation. That is, the tax accountant or tax lawyer has studied the behavior of taxpayers in their natural environment and is able to predict better how taxpayers might behave in various situations.

When it comes to knowing or predicting things about taxation, the clinical knowledge of tax practitioners should nearly always be considered a superior method to the imaginary models proposed by economists. Tax practitioners have usually thought about the various ways their clients might engage in tax avoidance. So, if an economist sits in a room with a tax lawyer and accountant and says, "Let's just design tax policy to not have large corporations or the wealthy pay any taxes, wouldn't that be great?" then the tax expert knows better. A tax expert might say in response: "What makes you think the wealthy pay any taxes now? None of my rich clients pay much tax. My salary, though, is taxed at a confiscatory rate. If we don't tax the wealthy, will you tax me even more on my salary? Who will make up the difference? Is the federal government going to borrow more money? Perhaps the government plans to cut back on its expenditures—I doubt it. Your proposal doesn't seem fair or efficient." If tax practitioners as a group were allowed to participate in tax policy discussions, the tax practitioners would certainly be the adults in the room when economists first served up tax policy proposals to the president.

It will be helpful here to provide illustrations of other things tax practitioners are likely to remember from experience. All of these particular illustrations are what I refer to as paradoxes in tax policy—situations in which common sense about taxes and tax rates does not comport to practical experience. This is important because famous professors at prestigious law schools have proposed that tax policy is simple and tax policy should be based on common sense.

Policymakers too believe that tax policy is simple and base their decisions on intuition and gut instinct. This isn't so and that methodology of supposedly knowing things about taxation and tax policy through gross simplifications is flawed and doesn't work in practice. The idea that tax is simple is catastrophically wrong and harmful to the future development of mankind—even more harmful than using imaginary economic models to formulate tax policy in my estimation. In any case, here are some illustrations of tax paradoxes that are obvious to those who ply the tax trade, indicating that tax policy is not so simple, but perhaps surprising to those without clinical knowledge of taxation:

- *Capital expenditures are tax deductible to businesses.* Large corporations can effectively choose how much income tax they will pay by deciding whether they want to reinvest profits into the business. Historically, large corporations have chosen not to reinvest profits and instead to buy back stock.[3] The lack of reinvestment makes it possible for the large corporation to pay some income tax. On the other hand, if corporations reinvested enough capital this reinvestment could wipe out their current tax liabilities irrespective of the tax rate. Of course, that degree of capital reinvestment would be good for the economy and should be considered desirable. As a tax policy matter, this also means that if a large corporation runs its business like an annuity without making any reinvestment, and then complains about its potential liability for income tax, the appropriate response is not to reduce the tax rate, but to say: "Why don't you reinvest some profits into a new business line? If you do, the capital expenditures will shelter your current profits from the income tax." Therefore, the income tax system itself serves to encourage capital reinvestment by currently profitable firms by offering a tax deduction for new capital investment to expand existing business lines or start new businesses. The tax deductions can be taken either currently by expense, as is often the case, or over time in the form of depreciation or amortization. The tax liability of firms that start new businesses will be less than the tax liability of firms that operate as an annuity and do not reinvest profits into new business ventures. This is part of the reason capitalism works well to encourage new business formation. Capitalism does not work as well if the tax rates are set too low because this reduces the value of tax deductions to firms that are already profitable. Low tax rates encourage large corporations to run their businesses like annuities by accumulating profits and not reinvesting profits into new business ventures.
- *Wealthy people don't actually pay taxes.* Leona Helmsley said it best: "We don't pay taxes. Only the little people pay taxes." That's basically correct, but it's also counterintuitive. The income tax system in the United States has a

progressive rate structure, but overall it is regressive when all taxes are taken into account, and by a wide margin. Lower-income persons pay an effective tax rate multiples higher than the wealthy. I illustrated this a few years ago by a mathematical calculation of a comprehensive effective tax rate;[4] the regressivity can also be explained qualitatively as follows: First, income taxes are just one of many tax types, and the other taxes (besides income taxes) are disproportionately paid by lower-income persons. Examples of other taxes are wage taxes, property taxes (often included in high rents), sales taxes, gasoline taxes and fees for mandatory government services. When all tax types are taken into account, the other types of taxes also paid by the poor cause the system to become regressive. Second, wage taxes are typically levied on a regressive basis. In the United States, a threshold applies on wage taxes, and earnings above that threshold are not subject to Social Security tax.[5] Income tax is also levied on wage earnings—even the portion withheld to pay the wage taxes. This is to say there is no deduction for wage taxes paid in assessing the income tax. So, money is withheld from the worker's paycheck, and then the worker is asked to pay income taxes on the withheld money, which the worker never received. A double taxation obviously results in the second layer of taxation of a portion of the wage earnings, which leads to a high effective tax rate on labor income.[6] The aggregate amount is more than any other form of the so-called double tax within the tax system, such as the corporate tax. Third, the progressive income tax rates apply on taxable income, not gross income. Taxable income includes income after all deductions. Wage income is generally not reduced by deductions and is taxed as the earnings accrue to the worker each year.

- *Tax deferral is more important than the statutory tax rate.* In the actual practice of taxation, tax professionals seek to delay the levy of tax on their clients—that attempt to delay taxation is often the primary objective and not to defeat the tax outright. With respect to capital assets, gains are not taxed on an accrual basis, which means that the holder of the capital asset may choose whether and when to recognize a gain. The Statutory Tax Rate is therefore not the only variable relevant to calculation of tax as there is also a Tax Base. This can be explained by the formula: Tax Base × Statutory Tax Rate = Tax Assessment.[7] See the difference from what you've heard on television? There are actually two variables that determine the taxes to be paid: statutory tax rate and taxable base. You need to know the taxable base to discuss whether tax rates are too high. As a general rule, wealthy people and large corporations are concerned with reducing the taxable base in many different ways. Poor people and working people are more concerned with the statutory tax rate.

Labor income is rarely deferrable, so if you have earned income you pay tax on it today at very high rates. That's the foremost secret of the tax system, although it's an open secret—and it's a realization that every tax practitioner has to master somewhere along the way to becoming a competent tax advisor.

ECONOMIC MODELS IN THE PRESIDENTIAL BRIEF

Economic models posit an imaginary universe that may or may not relate to the actual world. Tax policy is derived for that imaginary universe in economic theory, not the actual world, and the imaginary universe selected by economists reflects their biases and preferences. Competing economists can even disagree with each other by positing alternative models, essentially to posit a different functioning of the tax system on Jupiter as in comparison to Mars. This is why Karl Popper said that nonexistential statements are not scientific and therefore cannot be considered in the nature of true "science." Anything could be true in the imaginary universes on Jupiter and Mars, including that wealthy people and large corporations actually pay significant amounts of taxes on those planets, or that statutory tax rates can be used as a proxy instead of effective tax rates to determine the efficiency effects of tax policy, or even that taxes could be cut and more money collected along the lines of the Laffer curve.

The physics in the imaginary worlds of these equations always presumes that tax cuts for the wealthy or large corporations cause economic growth and, even more importantly, that requiring workers to pay taxes does not harm economic growth. The imaginary universes of economics always agree on these premises. The field of tax policy is thus largely the process of judging whether different imaginary hypotheticals are better or worse at achieving the implicit goal of economics, which is to tax workers to the maximum extent possible. In these simplified imaginary worlds, the Greek letters could be arranged in various ways to estimate different degrees of economic growth that would result, for example, if we allocated corporations an ever larger and larger share of profits. It is important to remember this: there is no empirical evidence derived from the actual world behind any of these imaginings that economists first propose out of thin air and then debate with one another.

Now, there are some obvious practical problems with the application of this epistemological method in the formation of tax policy. One problem is that the people who know better than economists about how the tax system works—especially tax accountants and lawyers, or members of what I refer to as the "professional tax guild"—are nowhere to be found in the initial presidential briefing. Tax accountants and lawyers are also not reviewers for the academic economic journals where tax policy ideas first emerge. Hence, there is no check on whether the imagination of the economist matches the reality of the actual world as it is. In the best of circumstances, matching the imagination to the actual world is an inductive process of choice between various imaginings that could never be "science" as Popper described it. That is, we would say that there is no way to know if economic theories about tax policy are right or wrong, and I would even say cynically from long experience in the field that nobody really wants to know either.

Even if the economic process of rearranging Greek letters is itself a deductive process, deciding whether the letters match the world is an inductive process, so nothing about economics could constitute science or scientific inquiry—at least, as the term *science* is understood in the hard sciences, like biology, physics and astronomy. Economic inquiry that puts forward a model is not science because it comprises neither theory nor empirical evidence nor any attempt to create a theory or gather evidence to support the proposed economic model. Typically, economists who believe themselves to be "experts" in tax policy started out as PhD students and were encouraged in their younger years to sit in their office and create imaginary models about the economy. Almost never did an economist advise a client about taxes, such as how to defer taxation, for example. This means that economists lack practical knowledge about the functioning of the tax system. Practical knowledge derived from advising clients about taxation is "clinical" tax knowledge, similar to clinical knowledge of medical doctors who, for example, see opioid abuse in the real world and then learn how it affects people. Of course, tax lawyers and tax accountants advise real businesses and real people on tax matters every day. So, economists writing about and advising on tax policy have typically no clinical knowledge about taxation—all of their knowledge is hypothetical, conjured while sitting in an office somewhere. The people who do have clinical knowledge about taxation are largely not involved in the process of advising the president or Congress on tax policy.

The experts in the professional tax guild wait in the wings to see what comes out of the meeting between the economist and the president and how they can profit by it. But since economic theory is imaginary, it's very difficult to predict what might happen. As an example, one economist might imagine the Laffer curve predominates on Jupiter, and another economist might posit a deadweight loss on Mars, and both would certainly say that their particular ideas are best suited to understanding tax policy here on Earth. For people that don't have clinical knowledge about taxation, really anything might be true (and anything is possible) in terms of tax policy. The only limit is the economist's imagination. It follows that if a professional tax advisor wishes to maximize profit from the tax system, it makes sense to wait and see what the economist will imagine about tax policy and then see what the president will do or accept in the initial policy briefing.

TAX CONTENT IN THE PRESIDENTIAL BRIEF

The primary purpose of the initial policy briefing is to guide the president on economic policy and begin to transition from campaigning to actual governance. In terms of taxes and tax policy, this usually means beginning to coax the president to think in terms of aggregate tax receipts, rather than in terms of statutory tax rates that may apply to wealthy individuals and corporations. This is not necessarily an easy transition, as statutory tax rates often form the backdrop to campaign debates. While a candidate for national political office, the president may have spent significant time studying the tax rates, mostly to avoid a factual misstatement that would be interpreted as an embarrassing mistake during the course of a debate.

But the president quickly finds that this type of politicized information about statutory tax rates is really not very helpful once in office. The objective of the first briefing is thus to provide the president with information on where the money comes from in order to run the federal government. The chief economist faces the difficult task of transitioning discussions of tax policy, mostly rhetoric and often in terms of efficiency or fairness, to more practical topics such as how much each tax type generates in receipts and so forth. The formulation of tax policy is very different from merely speaking persuasively about tax policy, since some background knowledge on the taxes actually collected by the federal government is a prerequisite. In summary, the initial policy briefing to the president, regardless of the president's political affiliation, sets out to describe the origins and amounts of tax receipts that constitute the sources of funding for the federal government. Of course, another source of federal funds is governmental borrowing.

There are two primary topics that the initial economic brief to the president entails. One of these topics relates to tax policy and is broadly the subject of this book. The other topic dealing with monetary policy and the Federal Reserve which has been debated by economists since the time of John Maynard Keynes. The latter topic of monetary policy refers of course to the setting of interest rates on government borrowings, which is done by the Federal Reserve Board. It's possible that the president could—and probably should as a practical matter—invite the chairman of the Federal Reserve to the initial economic briefing. But that is probably unlikely for various practical reasons. In any case, the first thing the president is told in the economic brief is that the trend in interest rates is crucial to economic growth—if interest rates are in the process of being cut, this is good for the economy, and if interest rates are in the process of being raised, this is bad.

As important to this book, the *second thing* the president is told relates directly to taxation and is that most of the federal budget is derived from taxing workers by taking money directly out of worker paychecks, either through payroll tax or income tax on earned income. At the time of the election of President Trump, the actual tax figures would have been somewhere north of 82 percent of federal tax receipts arising directly from various forms of worker taxes.[8] But given the reductions in tax rates in the Tax Cuts and Jobs Act of 2017, designed to reduce the taxes of nearly everyone except workers, the figures are today something like 90 percent, perhaps even higher. In fact, the taxes on workers are so high that the federal government historically borrowed out of the Social Security trust fund to fund the federal budget. Economists justify this system defined by the high tax on workers by saying that the Baby Boomer generation has more people than later generations, so the taxes need to be set high enough to build a surplus. Then, to the next generation, economists say that the wage taxes need to be high to make up the shortfall required to pay for the Baby Boomers as a larger group. Then economists will say to the subsequent generation that the wage taxes need to be even higher or the system will collapse. So, the sky is always falling and therefore workers have to pay high taxes. This sky-is-falling approach to justify worker taxes will continue indefinitely with new justifications invented anew for each subsequent generation and forward indefinitely into the future.

Nonetheless, the president's first realization, or really that of any politician when confronted with the reality of the tax system, is that workers pay nearly all the taxes in the United States, and this probably comes as a shock upon assuming the office. This is because political discourse on tax policy is premised on nonsense that only the rich and large corporations pay income taxes. However, all of that nonsense goes out the window during the first presidential brief on the sources of federal revenue, when tax policy is actually reduced to numbers. Notably, the president and the chief economic advisor really have no choice but to reduce tax policy to numbers as soon as the president takes on the role of chief executive and attempts to set policy. However, it goes without saying that speaking about taxes and tax policy in terms of numbers is extremely inconvenient, and also intellectually difficult, especially for those who have become immersed in political and ideological debates on the topic of taxation and may have come to actually believe the rhetoric.

IDEOLOGY IN THE PRESIDENTIAL BRIEF

An excellent book about the ideology of taxation was written by Louis Eisenstein more than fifty years ago, *The Ideologies of Taxation*.[9] Eisenstein describes the political process of debating taxation in political terms. My parallel interest in this current book is to set out an entirely different approach to our understanding of the tax system, and not so much to discuss ideology. In this book, I relate the theory of taxation to the actual world as it is, in which workers pay all, or nearly all, of the taxes, and thus not to an imaginary world of moral philosophy or economic models in which the wealthy and large corporations pay the imaginary taxes. That world isn't real when reduced to accounting terms. So I don't find it helpful to discuss the fairness or efficiency of tax policy in that imaginary universe when we discuss only statutory or marginal tax rates and thereby do not set out to account for who pays and who does not pay taxes. Fairness and efficiency have literally nothing to do with the formation of tax policy in the actual world. In fact, the tax system has been designed by economists mostly by following the teachings of the world's first economist, Thomas Malthus, in order to be categorically unfair and drastically inefficient. Accordingly, there is actually no plausible way that the tax system as currently designed can be described as either fair or efficient. Prior justifications suggesting that the tax system is fair contain accounting gimmicks and are premised on these gimmicks to make the fairness claims.

The proffering of a justification, any justification, for the unfairness and inefficiency in tax policy is actually *the point* of economic theory. The truth is that economics as a discipline arose because industrialists and factory owners wanted to buy what Malthus was selling during the Industrial Revolution. Malthus wrote:

> The labouring poor, to use a vulgar expression, seem always to live from hand to mouth. Their present wants employ their whole attention, and they seldom think of the future. Even when they have an opportunity of saving they seldom exercise it, but all that is beyond their present necessities goes, generally speaking, to the ale-house.[10]

Industrialists felt good reading that the poor were inferior and would not use any surplus wisely, so they paid Malthus to write and develop the field of economics to disseminate these ideas—and it worked and was wildly successful.

Factory workers, and especially children working in factories, died from the resulting privations until it became obvious to the British government that Malthusian theory would not work in practice, even over a short period of time, and the lack of subsistence wages rippled through society with disastrous social costs. The origin of economics was later intentionally and wrongly attributed to Adam Smith, in order to avoid association with Malthus (whose statistical predictions were disproved). But Malthus's underlying theories were still applied throughout nearly all economic thought—which to this day does not assign any value to the *social costs* of wage taxation.

Economic theory does assign various costs to other types of taxation (that should be understood as similar to or grouped with the "social costs" attributable to wage taxation), such as corporate tax or income tax levied on the wealthy. In the details of economic theorizing on tax policy, economists reveal that they have found reasons to count theoretical costs that supposedly arise from taxes on the wealthy, but never on the poor. This mismatch—saying that one type of tax creates a social cost and another does not—effectively resolves all questions of tax policy design from the very beginning. Accordingly, economists feel no pressing need to gather empirical evidence to support these Malthusian ideas. This is lucky for economists because the plain fact of the matter is that when Charles Dickens responded to Malthus many centuries ago, he was right: no empirical evidence will ever be found that economic thought on tax policy is accurate. In actual fact, there is nothing to economic theory in terms of tax policy, just a magician's simple flip of the cape, and all tax policy results are known and the poor are always required to pay the taxes. These conclusions are merely supposed to be efficient; there is no need for a whit of evidence that those Malthusian ideas even *might* be true.

Even though the attribution of the origins of economics to Smith instead of Malthus was successful, the modern theories of tax policy can be explained more readily by looking to Malthus's first ideas. One scholar explained the distinction without a difference as follows:

> Neo-classical economists adopted essentially the same position with respect to the harmful effects of poor relief, but their opposition was no longer based on Malthus's reasoning. They argued that the receipt of relief tended to undermine habits of industry and thrift among the poor, thereby reducing their productivity and consequently the wages they could command. The result was an account of poverty among able-bodied persons that supported essentially the same policy conclusion as Malthus, but with a focus on productivity rather than fertility.[11]

To the contrary, in terms of tax policy there is little or no identifiable difference between Malthus's writings and neoclassical economic theory as it stands today. The policy recommendations are always the same, either way. A Nobel Prize in economics was even awarded in 2017 to Richard Thaler partly for the idea of libertarian paternalism, which developed from his ideas.[12] As applied to taxation and tax policy, this oxymoron stands for the now widely held belief among economists that the poor are unable to make rational decisions on their own terms. Of course, the wealthy are presumed able to make rational decisions by their own terms.

For now, the key idea is that economists are so convinced of the superiority of their own ideas that they truly believe that the poor make irrational decisions and the wealthy do not. Is it possible that this is merely what the wealthy want to believe about the poor in order to justify their own irrationality and greed? I think so. With the push toward libertarian paternalism, economists have essentially set up a mirror and each time they move their own hand in order to describe the expected "rational" behavior, the figure in the mirror also moves in a similar way. However, when economists then look to see whether other people also move in that way which they expect to see from experience watching their own movements in the mirror, it turns out they don't, and economists then call that "irrational" behavior because it doesn't make sense to them. The trouble with this approach is not that other people don't act rationally but that economists simply don't understand what supposedly "rational" behavior means to other people.

The paternalist nature of the tax system is illustrated foremost by the idea of Pigouvian taxes. A Pigouvian tax is a tax levied to offset an externality that is attributable to a particular product or activity.[13] Yet, whenever lower-income persons use a product (whether gasoline, cigarettes, sugar or fast foods), economists argue that there are externalities that need to be offset using the tax system.[14] Where the wealthy use a harmful product (e.g., foie gras, private jet travel), economists raise no paternalist concern over *internalities*, as opposed to externalities.[15] The concept of *internality* refers to the costs to a person from the use of a product that the person does not take into account by their own standards. Of course, this is shorthand for "paternalism."[16] The double standard in the paternalist claims on Pigouvian taxes is palpable. Such arguments are proposed even where the existing taxes on the respective product already exceed every measure of the respective externality.

Likewise, in terms of tax policy today, wealthy people want to buy the moral philosophy that economic theory is selling. The basic rule in economic theorizing is to simply give the wealthy people, Leona Helmsley as a prime example, what they want in tax policy. Economics is simply giving the rich and powerful what the rich and powerful want to read or to imagine might be true, nothing more. The rich and powerful do not want a tax system that is fair and efficient because such a system would cause the economy to experience rapid and explosive growth by and through small business expansion. Why would small businesses expand? Because absent the design of the tax system as it is, so designed to pull every last dollar out of the hands of the aspiring entrepreneur or small business owner and thereby to prevent the growth of small business, small business would grow at an exponential rate. Second, the rich and powerful need to read things that justify inequality with bad outcomes for other persons (or, want to believe that such justifications exist even if they do not know or understand all the details)—where many of the suffering workers actually work for those very powerful people and are paid below subsistence wages. The justification is needed for the mental process of the wealthy to justify what they are doing to their own workers—this justification for doing obviously wrong things is entirely necessary to the functioning of the overall economic system.

PLAUSIBILITY OF THE PRESIDENTIAL BRIEF

An economic system designed to function essentially the opposite of how it is designed today—that is, *without* extremely high rates of tax on workers and small business, or by even allowing small business ready access to capital that would allow rapid economic expansion—should be expected to expand with ready capital availability for small businesses at a compounding rate approximating 10 percent or more per year. Rapid economic growth has occurred time and again throughout history, when small businesses have been allowed and encouraged to flourish. The intellectual problem is not really with how to design a tax system to best facilitate economic growth as economists generally believe, as that's easy and well-known based on prior human experience. If rapid economic growth is desirable, then the solution is simply to unleash small business with small influxes of capital investment. Small business owners will do the rest by the sweat of their brow combined with small amounts of capital. The real problem is that nobody seems to want rapid economic growth.

In the modern economy as it stands, small business activity has been suppressed. Small business has been largely eliminated as competition for large firms in the lines of business where large firms wish to operate through both the tax system and unfavorable trade policy; as a result, economic growth is essentially stagnant. The economy grows at a real rate of 0.5 percent or so, and economists pretend to push this upward to 2 percent or 3 percent by pretending that price inflation does not exist. But this is something that working people don't really believe—every consumer knows that the price for many types of consumer products seems to double every few years and that real wages never keep pace with the increased prices. Therefore, economic growth isn't real and reflects merely higher prices. The increased profits reflect the higher prices that companies have been able to charge their customers and that constitute inflation. In economic terms, what is being called "growth" is nominal growth, not real growth, where increases in prices charged must be reduced by inflation. The deception is simply not to subtract anything from reported figures of economic growth for price increases so that as prices go up, the government can pretend that nominal growth is economic growth, even though it absolutely is not.

Since the power to tax is the power to destroy,[17] the best way to keep the economy from growing quickly is to tax the heck out of workers and small business and thereby destroy these persons in economic terms. In the era of the Industrial Revolution in Britain, wrongdoers were killed even for minor property offenses. Today, wrongdoers who try to start a small business that might compete with large business are destroyed as competitors by having capital constantly removed from their hands. Any interference with big business is the primary form of "wrongdoing" today. Then, whatever legitimate business ideas the entrepreneur may have developed and tried to implement are squelched because of lack of capital, lawsuits by competitors and so on. Both economics and the moral philosophy of taxation are the justification for destroying working persons in every new generation through tax policy—that is what tax policy in the modern era serves to do as small business are subject to effective tax rates at least double, if not triple or quadruple, the effective tax rates paid by large multinational firms. Again, fairness and efficiency have nothing to do with tax policy or ideology as it currently stands. I return to the topic of tax ideology in subsequent paragraphs and later chapters.

If the economic system were redesigned so as to allow small business to expand—in other words, to allow capitalism to function—then people who are now poor would become rich, and some people who are now rich might become poor, or, might become at least not as rich as they could have been in relative terms. Above all else, the owners of large businesses do not want that explosive growth of small business activity to happen; today's wealthy also don't want that to happen because it would change their *rank order in wealth holdings*. Richard Epstein has spoken to the wealthy about their great fear of rapid changes in the rank-ordering of persons in society.[18] I agree at least on the identification of that concern as the primary element of moral philosophy as applied to taxation. The fear given voice by Epstein is that tax policy might itself cause changes in the rank-orderings of person by redistribution of wealth, or even merely allow such changes to happen through the expansion of small business activity. Notably, in the time of the Enlightenment, with both slavery and widespread indentured servitude, any such changes in social standing were frightening to the upper classes. Today, increases in economic inequality motivate similar fears in the upper classes, as a not-entirely-unreasonable concern over one's spendthrift children falling down into the abyss of poverty, creates an insatiable need for more wealth accumulation. In that way, wealth accumulation satiates the need that was previously served by hereditary title in the noble classes, which is no longer viable. Accordingly, the avoidance of any possibility of change in social standing or changes in the rank-ordering of persons in society is the primary goal of tax policy informed by moral philosophy. It follows that tax policy actually becomes the foremost means to defeat the American dream. And, it is predominantly tax policy, as much as any other factor, that explains why the American dream is dead.

WHY TAX POLICY IS THE WAY IT IS

The last few sections are likely to be interpreted as bad news by any president for two reasons: First, it turns out that the chairman of the Federal Reserve adjusts interest rates and sets monetary policy, not the president directly. Second, because the source of federal revenue is nearly entirely the taxation of workers, the president really does not directly control tax collections either, and the president does not even *indirectly* control tax collections through influencing congressional legislation. Rather, the collection of tax receipts from workers that accounts for the vast majority of federal revenue, necessary to fund everything the federal government does, operates essentially on autopilot. The first presidential brief on economic policy, then, is a wake-up call on the limits of what the president can do on tax and economic policy, both in constitutional terms and in practical economic terms. The first lesson: the president does not do much. That means that the president who wishes to foster economic growth through policy reform, in order to facilitate reelection, may not see a ready path to accomplish this objective. The policy briefing is likely to result in frustration as the president realizes that he or she may not be able to cause the economic change thought to be possible during the course of the election. The chief economic advisor will be aware of this potential for frustration in conducting the initial brief on tax policy. This lack of potential to facilitate change may even have partly motivated the individual to seek out the office of the presidency, so this first brief on economic and tax policy is likely to be *terribly* frustrating.[19]

Now, it is possible to better explain generally why tax policy is the way it is. In the initial brief, the president is told the following either explicitly or in a nutshell:

Economic Directive 1. By the actual numbers, workers remit most (nearly all) taxes in one form or another.

Economic Directive 2. If the president does anything to cause workers to pay less tax, the federal government will become insolvent, the system will fail, and everything will collapse. The legacy of a president who cuts taxes for workers will be having the honor of being the last president before the economic collapse. (Of course, this isn't true, but it is what economists can be expected to advise the president.)

Economic Directive 3. If the president chooses to cut taxes for the wealthy or large corporations, the standard economic "model" says that the economy will grow much faster and everyone will be more prosperous, including workers. (Again, this isn't true, but we can be sure the current president has been told as much and future presidents will also be wrongly so advised.)

Economic Directive 4. The poor as a class waste nearly all of their surplus money "in the ale-house," as Malthus said. Accordingly, the poor need to be taught a lesson about "rational" economic behavior. And, the tax system is an ideal opportunity to teach the poor a lesson. So through extremely high tax rates on labor income, the poor will not have as much money to spend on vice —or anything else, and over the long-term this will be beneficial to society because the poor will be converted into capitalists and then able to enjoy the prosperity of the United States.

In the next chapter, the lack of a scientific basis for tax research will be explained. Deceptions within tax policy are made possible by the lack of scientific methods in tax research. For example, in any scientific version of tax policy, one would need to take into account the social costs of high rates of wage taxation.

NOTES

1 Victor Canto, Douglas Joines & Arthur Laffer, Tax Rates, Factor Employment, and Market Production, in *The Supply-Side Effects of Economic Policy*, ed. L. H. Meyer, 3–32 (Netherlands: Springer, 1981).

2 Karl Popper, *Realism and the Aim of Science*, ed. W. Bartley III (London: Routledge; New York, Taylor and Francis, 1983), at xix–xxi ("(4) Purely existential statements are not falsifiable [...] 'There is a ceremony whose exact performance forces the devil

to appear.' Such statements are not falsifiable. (They are, in principle, verifiable: it is logically possible to find a ceremony whose performance leads to the appearance of a human-like form with horns and hooves. And if a repetition of the ceremony fails to achieve the same result, that would be no falsification, for perhaps an unnoticed yet essential aspect of the correct ceremony was omitted.)").

3 Scott Lehtonen, *After $ 1 Trillion in Stock Buyback Spending, Companies Keep Their Wallets Open*, Investor's Business Daily (Jan. 12, 2019); Julia La Roche, *Corporate Stock Buybacks Are Booming*, Yahoo Finance (Feb. 20, 2019), https://finance.yahoo.com/news/corporate-stock-buybacks-rise-schumer-sanders-172223775.html. Accessed Nov 10, 2019.

4 Bret N. Bogenschneider, *The Effective Tax Rate of U.S. Persons by Income Level*, 145 TAX NOTES 117 (2014).

5 The maximum taxable earnings for Social Security withholding for 2019 are $132,900. IRS, Notice 1036, Internal Revenue Service (Dec. 2018), https://www.irs.gov/pub/irs-pdf/n1036.pdf.

6 See Robert Bellafiore, *The U.S. Tax Burden on Labor*, 2019, Tax Foundation (May 23, 2019), https://taxfoundation.org/us-tax-burden-on-labor-2019/; see also Jay Soled & Kathleen DeLaney Thomas, *Automation and the Income Tax*, 10:1 COLUMBIA J. OF TAX LAW, 1, 7–17 (2019) ("Labor income bears the nation's highest tax burden, which is largely attributable to the fact that it is taxed twice. First, the Code imposes an income tax on labor earnings. [...] Second, upon the very same earned income, the Code imposes employee and employer payroll taxes, which amount to an additional tax burden of roughly 15 percent.") (at 8, citations omitted).

7 See Brian Spilker et al., *Taxation of Individuals and Business Entities* (New York: McGraw Hill, 2020), at 1–9.

8 U.S. Treasury Department data on Federal Tax Revenues (Fiscal Year 2017).

9 Louis Eisenstein, *The Ideologies of Taxation* (Cambridge: Harvard University Press, 1961).

10 John Avery, *Malthus' Essay on the Principle of Population* (Denmark: University of Copenhagen, 2005), at 27.

11 See Philip Harvey, *Joblessness and the Law Before the New Deal*, 6 GEO. J. POVERTY L. & POL'Y 1, 27 (1999).

12 Richard Thaler & Cass Sunstein, *Libertarian Paternalism*, 93 AMERICAN ECONOMIC REVIEW 175 (2003).

13 See J. Masur & E. Posner, *Toward a Pigouvian State*, 164 U. PA. L. REV. 93 (2015); but see V. Fleischer, *Curb Your Enthusiasm for Pigovian Taxes*, 68 VAND. L. REV. 1673 (2015).

14 See, e.g., Kelly Brownell et al., *The Public Health and Economic Benefits of Taxing Sugar-Sweetened Beverages*, 361 N. ENGL. J. MED. 1599 (2009).

15 See Bret Bogenschneider, *A "Fool" and His Sugar Sweetened Beverage Are Soon Taxed*, 38 LIVERPOOL L. REV. 1, 18 (2017) ("In terms of particular food products, what about gout-causing *foie gras* consumed primarily by the wealthy? Well, presumably, under the approach of Brownell, et al., the taxation should be maximized to stop the wealthy from harming themselves by consuming the *foie gras* product. The bottom line is that the link between Libertarian Paternalism and any particular tax policy and the specific consumer items upon which the policy is to be applied, at least thus far seems to be solely the class of the person making the purchase decision.").

16 See David Adam Friedman, *Public Health Regulation and the Limits of Paternalism*, 46 CONN. L. REV. 1687 (2013).

17 *McColloch v. Maryland*, 17 U.S. (4 Wheat.) 316 (1819), 427 ("That the power of taxing [...] by the States may be exercised so as to destroy it, is too obvious to be denied"; Daniel Webster, oral argument: "An unlimited power to tax involves, necessarily, a power to destroy," 17 U.S. at 327.

18 Richard A. Epstein, *Taxation in a Lockean World*, 4:1 SOC. PHIL. & POL. 49 (1986). Various articles have identified that tax "equity" can be described in terms of rank-ordering reversals caused by the tax system. See Daniel Attas, *Fragmenting Property*, 25 LAW & PHIL. 119 (2006); A. B. Atkinson, Horizontal Equity and the Distribution of the Tax Burden, in *The Economics of Taxation* (Washington, DC: Brookings Institute, 1980); Robert Plotnick, *A Measure of Horizontal Inequity*, 63 REV. ECON. & STAT. 283 (1981).

19 See Heather Long, *Goldman Sachs Predicts Only Minor Boost From Trump's Tax Cuts*, Washington Post (Oct. 9, 2016), https://www.washingtonpost.com/news/wonk/wp/2017/10/09/goldman-sachs-predicts-dinky-boost-from-trumps-tax-cuts/. Accessed Nov 10, 2019.

CHAPTER 2

THE ABANDONMENT OF SCIENTIFIC METHODS IN TAX RESEARCH

Chapter Summary: *Tax policy is generally not formulated with the aid of science or scientific methods. Shockingly little attempt is made by professional tax scholars to gather evidence in order to test accepted theories of causation using empirical data. If obviously contrary data is identified from practical experience, as derived from observable changes in tax policy, such as what occurred with the corporate tax cuts of 2017, for example, it is simply ignored. Accordingly, tax theories are almost never updated in light of contrary evidence. Instead, economic "models" are often used on an exclusive basis to formulate tax policy. Such models should be considered nonscience because, even though some of them involve logical deduction as a means of knowing, they still rely on induction as a means of the choice of model. Other tax scholars, especially lawyers, propose simplified ideas of tax policy based on their moral beliefs about whether tax policies are right or wrong. This "common sense" means of knowing things reflects an approach that is essentially a premodern epistemology and the opposite of scientific inquiry. Such a premodern way of knowing things about tax policy dates all the way back to the mid-1600s. There are many reasons for today's haphazard, nonscientific and even premodern approach to tax policy; for example, it is indeed much easier to deceive taxpayers using these methods than it is using more modern views premised on science. In fact, tax policy is an extraordinarily complex field of social inquiry to which modern science and epistemology are well suited. There is simply no reason to not apply scientific methods in tax research.*

If it is true that tax policy is based on mostly deception, as I suggested was the case in Chapter 1, then many additional questions arise including whether we humans know anything at all about taxation and tax policy? So, we should ask ourselves what do we know for sure about tax? How do we know what we don't know? Are scientific methods reflected in tax research? Would the use of science potentially help us avoid further deceptions? If so, why do tax scholars not insist on the use of science in conducting tax research? How would we even go about *scientific* tax research? What might the results be if tax policy was formulated in a scientific manner?

Lucky for tax scholars, they can draw on all of human experience as the methodology of science has undergone a type of continuous improvement in each new era, from the classical era and Roman times, to the Enlightenment era and colonial times, and since the beginning of the Modern era in the early 1900s. With each new era humans improved the methods of knowing things, and those improved methods can help us answer our questions on taxation and tax policy in a consistent way. So, to answer the question of whether scientific methods are currently used in tax research, it is necessary to place tax theory on the progression of scientific inquiry.

Tax theory as we know it today began during the Enlightenment era and, importantly, the discipline of taxation has continued to apply the methods of the Enlightenment era to the present day, even for specific tax policies. For example, a crucial element of Enlightenment-era thinking was the rank-ordering of persons by the amount of acreage or slaves held. The modern-day system still maintains that rank-ordering—except that they are now measured by wealth. Before that, the ancient Romans of the classical era had tax types that resemble the value-added tax—or VAT—which are still found across Europe today. Many of the current ideas about tax date back to the Enlightenment-era writings of Adam Smith and the publication of his book *The Wealth of Nations* in 1776. The idea of science, though, as it applied to economic theory in Adam Smith's time is premodern science. Even today, roughly 250 years after Adam Smith and the Enlightenment era, some of our tax concepts and policies are not enlightened. It was only during the subsequent Modernist period of the early 1900s that current ideas of science and scientific methods originated, as well as the development of the philosophy of science, that might allow for the development of a Modernist version of tax policy. The following sections on the philosophy of science delve into how people might know or come to know things about taxation and tax policy using science or the scientific method.

What is a theory of "knowing"?

Answer: Epistemology. Epistemology simply refers to a consistent way of deciding how to know things. The best example of an "epistemology" is the scientific method.

Where do we look to determine what it means to "know"?

Answer: Our current understanding of science and scientific inquiry (as opposed to taxation and tax policy) is premised on developments in the early 1900s when the philosophy of science originated. The philosophy of science is a means of *knowing* premised on methods for updating beliefs based on evidence. Accordingly, a proper scientist would insist on the origin of knowledge in method, and thus not insist on the holding of certain beliefs as incontrovertible truths as in religion—obviously, in tax policy nearly all discourse is premised on the holding of certain incontrovertible truths. These inconvertible truths are now often given under the guise of economics or "common sense."

How does the current understanding of philosophy of science suggest that humans "know" things about tax or anything else?

Answer: Science "knows" through the use of testable theories of cause and effect. A theory of causation is often tested with data or other evidence. If other scientists are not able to replicate results of a theory as proposed, then it is usually rejected or sometimes modified to yield better results. If a theory is really good, then this means that other scientists are not able to design an experiment to disprove the causal predictions of the theory. Karl Popper referred to the process of selection as between scientific theories as similar to a process of natural selection.[1]

Do ideas about taxation currently include testable theories of cause and effect?

Answer: Absolutely not. It is unclear whether modern ideas about taxation and tax policy include even one single testable theory of cause and effect that might be considered along the lines of accepted "science" or scientific methods. For example, economic theory given in respect of taxation is almost exclusively a series of justifications for the taxation of workers and only studies that tend to support that justification can be published in economic journals. For example, other hypotheses, such as the potential that tax reductions on workers might create efficiency gains for society, may indeed exist, but these have never been published or tested using numbers in any prominent economic journal, at least to the knowledge of the author, and will never be published because the editors simply will not allow it to happen.

If tax ideas don't include testable theories of cause and effect, then where does tax "knowledge" come from?

Answer: Tax ideas come mainly from prior understandings of epistemology taken from the seventeenth (the 1600s) and eighteenth (the 1700s) centuries or even earlier. In fact, most beliefs about tax policy are derived from economics, and the field of economics uses ideas originating mainly in the Enlightenment era of the late 1700s. In nearly all other fields of science and social science—apart from taxation—Enlightenment-era ideas have been updated and replaced to align with modern times and Modernist views taken from the 1900s, and even postmodern ideas arising in the late 1950s to the present day.

Are mankind's ideas about taxation thus still roughly the same as they were in the late 1600s and early to mid-1700s?

Answer: Yes. If you look to the tax literature, most scholars reach their conclusions by citing moral philosophy written in the mid-1700s, such as that of Jeremy Bentham, Adam Smith and John Stuart Mill. The first and leading economist of all time is of course Thomas Malthus, but modern-day economists are embarrassed to cite him (even though they often indirectly refer to his ideas and assumptions) because he is thought to have justified population control for the working classes. In the 1980s, the philosopher John Rawls further developed a new theory of liberalism that the academic tax community lauded in the tax context. Yet Rawls's ideas were stuck in a prior era—the Enlightenment—and scholars were simply celebrating a new way to do old philosophy and apply it to taxation.

Is there a progression (or timeline) of mankind's understanding of scientific inquiry? Where does tax knowledge fall along that progression of science?

Answer: Yes. The philosophy of science can be understood as a timeline in three stages: (1) premodern, or an organized system of defensible beliefs about taxation often premised mostly on established traditions and sometimes religion; (2) modernist, incorporating a means to gather evidence and test whether a belief that is thought to be true might not be true, such as by the scientific method and (3) postmodern, or a formal challenge to both the traditional means and the epistemological means of knowing things about taxation, and often suggesting that knowledge is based on power relations in society. Our present formation of tax policy and theory of taxation is largely stuck in the premodern stage. However, tax scholars in other nations, such as the United Kingdom, sometimes advance Modern theory in the context of tax policy.

A primary thesis of this book is that tax policy needs to progress from the premodern stage of human development where it is now stuck, to the modernist stage and in doing so it must reasonably withstand a postmodern critique. To do so, a revised version of tax policy must be based on something more than power relations in society, or the wielding of raw power by one group against another group, such as the rich against the poor, or vice versa. A premodern approach premised on moral philosophy derived from the Enlightenment era, where the wealthy carefully describe tax "fairness" in terms of maintaining rank-orderings of persons in property or slave holdings, for example, has no chance of withstanding a postmodern critique. If the philosophy of taxation is found to be merely a series of justifications for a system that favors the powerful in society, then that is not so much proper philosophy as it is the musings of the ruling class on tax matters. A philosopher would simply say that these types of moral justifications of the tax system were unable to withstand a postmodern critique.

But, the discipline of economics has developed lots of new terms for tax concepts over the past century, such as deadweight loss, Pareto optimality and so on. Doesn't that indicate economic knowledge about taxation has advanced from the 1600s because we have explanations for tax policy?

Answer: No, for two reasons. First, none of those new economic words are causal theories. We have only broad claims to the "trickle down" benefits of tax cuts as a causal theory—easily disproven and shown not to be true with basic statistics. Hence, they are not modern "scientific" methods of analysis as the causal method of analysis has been abandoned as unworkable within economic theory. Science and scientific inquiry were understood along these economic lines of justification by humans all the way through the 1600s, 1700s and even 1800s, as compared to the current time. It was only in the early 1900s that mankind's understanding of "science" shifted toward testable theories of cause and effect. This is how we understand "science" today. However, economics still uses the outdated conception of science taken from the 1600s. In economic methods it is not expected or considered necessary for a tax scholar to state a theory of cause and effect and to then subject it to testing with evidence or data. Second, the tax policy recommendations from the 1600s are always the same—tax the workers, peasants or lower classes— irrespective of differences in research methodology that might have been applied. This synchronicity of result strongly indicates the entire endeavor was a farce from the beginning. Tax experts continue to propose these same policy recommendations based on the outdated methods from that earlier time. So, any distinction in research methods within economics is really a distinction without a difference.

Economists seem to prepare long equations composed of Greek letters and then claim to "know" the tax policy result from the equation. So, that method seems very different than philosophical writings from the seventeenth century. In fact, economists only started using this equation method in late nineteenth and early twentieth centuries. Econometric analysis arose around the year 1890. I really don't see any similarity between the equation method and moral philosophy. What gives?

Answer: An approach to tax policy based on either imagined models (the equations) or Enlightenment standards of morality fails to state a causal "theory" that would be considered scientific inquiry. This is why economists never admit to being wrong (remember Arthur Laffer and his Laffer curve?), and it is also why economists can never be proved wrong by data that is acquired through experience. The statement of a scientific theory is a claim to what is and opens up the possibility of being wrong about what is—and science requires that possibility. Karl Popper, probably the most famous philosopher of science, described a key element of science as testability, because the possibility of being wrong is actually a compliment to any scientific theory. Another helpful description of science versus pseudoscience is from the archaeologist Kenneth Feder:

> Science and Nonscience: The Essential Differences. Through objective observation and analysis, a scientist, whether a physicist, chemist, psychologist, or archaeologist, sees things that need explaining. Through creativity and imagination, the scientist suggests possible hypotheses to explain these "mysteries." [...] If the implications of a hypothesis are shown not to be true, the hypothesis must be rejected [...] [A] hypothesis, whether it turns out to be upheld or not, to be scientific, it must be testable. In other words, there must be clear, deduced implications that can be drawn from the hypothesis and then tested.[2]

Any modern-day scientist, then, would be embarrassed to speak in the certain terms of economics, where scholars claim that aspects of tax policy—such as, say, that corporate tax cuts result in economic growth—are sure and incontrovertible truths.

So, economists on television who claim to know something for sure really are just revealing that economics is not based on modern science?

Answer: Exactly right. Economic "models" represent a simplified version of the world in which—only in that world—the economist does indeed know how the model operates and then can say things for sure. However, the actual economic world does not match to that simplified version of the world represented in the model. The comparison of the simplified world to the actual world is an "inductive" process, not a deductive one. This is the key logical point that some econometricians misunderstand. In their models composed of long strings of Greek letters and logical operands, economists deduce things only about the simplified universe of the model, and not the actual world. Economists using models are often confused because they analyze the Greek letters deductively and therefore think they "know" things about taxation for sure, by deduction, but they don't really. The reason for that is the two worlds don't necessarily match—economics has only deduced things about the alternate or simplified universe depicted in the "model." The choice between alternative universes represented in various models that economists may like or dislike is a matter of inductive reasoning only, and not deductive reasoning, even if the model within one universe operates entirely by deduction.

Doesn't all this critique mean we don't know anything about taxes and tax policy? And, never can know anything?

Answer: No. A scientist is someone that creates a "theory" and subjects the theory to testing using evidence. A good theory withstands all the tests that can be devised. For example, scientists hold the theory of gravity to be true because other scientists are unable to show that it is wrong through experiment or by finding a case where the theory does not hold and does not yield an accurate prediction. If gravity were not such a good theory, then we might expect humans to occasionally just float off into space, for example. In tax research, scholars should set out to develop theories about tax policy and then try to test whether those theories are true in the actual world. However, this has almost never been attempted in tax research. Our *scientific* knowledge about cause and effect in taxation and tax policy is nearly nonexistent.

But, isn't that process of what you refer to as "science" exactly what economists are doing by saying that it is always efficient to tax workers? Isn't that just a theory about tax policy?

Answer: No. The economic model that says that it is always efficient to tax workers is not a theory of causation. That economic model mainly justifies a tax policy result and does not make a prediction. The lack of any causal theory within these economic ideas about taxation should be obvious. For example, with respect to the taxation of workers, even as a matter of economic theory premised on supply of and demand for factors of production, efficiency must depend at least in part on which factor of production is in greater supply. For example, if labor is in short supply, and taxes reduce that supply even more, then it would not necessarily be efficient to tax labor, likely resulting in a further restriction of supply by taxation. By taxing labor which is already in short supply, production might drop or stop altogether—of course that would not be efficient. The incoherency within economics arises in that the justification for the taxation of labor represented within the economic theory is not a causal theory of supply and demand. Economists have simply claimed to "know" things about taxation and the efficiency of various tax policies, which they in fact did not know in causal terms, and the models are simply justifications. Economists selected specific models because they collectively liked the tax policy results from applying that particular model and not for any scientific reason.

Doesn't theoretical physics also use long equations and modeling, just the same as econometric analysis?

Answer: No. Theoretical physics always purports to be describing the actual world—even its discussions of alternate dimensions are all premised on the real world. Theoretical physicists—such as those who test their very advanced predictions at the Hadron collider in Switzerland—are excited about the *possibility* of testing a theory using the Hadron collider. That excitement about even the prospect of testing a theory is a hallmark of modern scientific inquiry. In contrast, economic models are nowhere near detailed enough to realistically describe the actual economy. Even a model that has, say, 20 economic variables can't come close to describing the countless variables that exist in the real world. Furthermore, the Federal Reserve has tried to replicate the econometric analyses of the world's top economists from the past 20 years, but was unable to do so most of the time.[3] So, econometrics is more like a hodgepodge of justification based on moral theories from various past historical eras that economists prefer for some reason—it is not science. In addition, economists are best described as recalcitrant toward the prospect of testing their current models of taxation used to formulate tax policy that is a hallmark of nonscientific inquiry.

Economists are smart people and claim to be discussing the real world! Are you saying economists don't know the difference between a model and the real world?

Answer: Sort of. The problem is that economists apply their models without testing them with data or other evidence. Scientific inquiry requires testing; whereas, in economic modeling testing is optional. Of course, lots of smart people are doing research in many fields without applying scientific methods or testing results. Yet, a person who claims to be a scientist and then never tests anything is simply not a true scientist no matter how smart or famous they are. At a minimum, the lack of testing of economic ideas makes it hard for other people to know whether to take such research seriously. The problem is partly that economists are so confident in their own intelligence they do not think that scientific methods are really necessary in the context of tax policy. Notably, in the premodern era, it actually was the case that people who did research were vastly more educated than the rest of society. But today, even if we assume that economists are smarter than everyone else, they still cannot be exempted from the methods of science. Tax policy couched in the credentials of an extremely famous and well-credentialed economist must still be subjected to testing! That testing is what the epistemology of science actually is and requires from its adherents. The testing of theories in the tax context is not optional even if such theory arises from an economic model derived from an extremely smart and famous economist that other economists believe and admire.

How would you propose to test a theory about economics if there are billions of variables, such as in respect of the modern-day economy with billions of people all making economic decisions?

Answer: A causal theory does not require billions of variables to be a valid scientific description of cause and effect. For example, a cause-and-effect economic theory could be this: A tax cut for wage earners will cause economic growth. This hypothesis would be refined over time to become more and more precise, so eventually, we might say precisely when and under which conditions that hypothesis can be held to be true. Economists today, instead of testing whether that hypothesis is true, attempt to build a scale model— but building a model of the real world is impossible because the real world has so many variables to consider. It would be like an astronomer who tries to build a scale model of the Milky Way galaxy out of metal and wood. As science gets more precise in its scope, then questions become more and more complex and refined, and it therefore becomes exponentially more difficult to build a scale model and build up "knowledge" from its foundations. Partly for this reason, modern science is premised more on theory than models.[4] And modern science, as opposed to scale models, can and should also be used to analyze competing theories of causation about taxation.

Sometimes researchers discover important things by accident, like penicillin. So what is this kind of research without theory if it's not science?

Answer: The scientific method is actually not the *only* way to conduct research, and there's no denying that scientists sometimes discover really important things by accident. But part of the reason science is the preferred methodology for research relates simply to efficiency. For example, anyone (or any computer) can make a haphazard guess, or a whole series of haphazard guesses, and begin to know things by narrowing down the scope of those guesses in order to not make the same wrong guess again. This would be trial-and-error research, like playing a game of Battleship. The problem is that it is radically inefficient to proceed in such a way—and moreover, even if a guess turns out to be correct, there is no explanation for *why* it is correct. In scientific inquiry, the person must be able to explain the *why* behind the guess in order to rule out mere coincidence and so define a causal link in science. Therefore, as part of the process of experimentation or testing, the statement of a causal hypothesis must be made first. If the hypothesis is stated after a test, then it might be taken as a case of the ends justifying the means—not as causation.

Where do causal theories come from in science?

Answer: The answer is not entirely clear. Both Karl Popper and Albert Einstein spoke on that very difficult question in their respective fields. The answer given by both was "creative intuition," translated from the German word: *Einfühlung*.[5] The field of economics, though, has made an extraordinary mistake with respect to epistemology. Economists have interpreted Popper's critique of inductive methods to mean that causal theories should be determined by deductive methods. That idea is wrong. Causal theories, or hypotheses, are to be evaluated by deduction where possible, but the origin of theory is creative intuition which is partly a type of abductive reasoning or reasoning by experience. The pertinent question, then, is who are the people likely to have creative intuition about matters of causation relevant to taxation and tax policy? The answer is practitioners or those people who have clinical, practical knowledge and experience in taxation, such as tax lawyers and accountants.[6]

What do you mean by the reference to "clinical" knowledge about tax law and accounting?

Answer: Clinical tax knowledge is the practical knowledge and experience of tax practitioners. Given their clinical knowledge and experience, tax practitioners ought to be considered good sources of hypotheses about taxation because they have experience with tax out in the world as it actually exists. This is similar to saying a nurse might be a good source of hypotheses about the causation of illness. If a tax practitioner identified a causal theory related to tax policy, that is a first step in a scientific method of inquiry. Economists, in contrast, have very little practical experience in taxation, which makes them less likely to formulate a meaningful theory of causation about taxation. Of course, it is possible to look at a data set and draw out a hypothesis from that data—an economist may be well suited to do that, but it is not science and does not reflect the scientific method. Searching for patterns in data sets is not scientific inquiry because many patterns exist in data sets and not all of them are causal. Thus, even if an economist searched through a data set and identified a pattern that seemed to be important, he or she would still need to check with a practitioner to see whether that pattern was meaningful. A pattern would only be found to be meaningful if it reflected some law or accounting method or change in the tax rules that was causing taxpayers to change their behavior in some way such that it then was found to be present in the respective data set.

Isn't social science different from physical science because humans make unpredictable choices?

Answer: Yes, of course. The unpredictability of the choices we make is referred to as *ergodicity*. Any theory of science related to taxation would be ergodic, which means that it is tentative and always subject to changes in human preferences about taxation. So, theories of cause and effect in economics and other social sciences can become even more difficult to develop and test than causal theories in the physical sciences because they have this aspect of ergodicity built into them.

Are common sense ideas a valid method of scientific inquiry in taxation?

Answer: One purpose of science and the scientific method is not to use "common-sense" as the method of knowing things about taxation. Scholars who describe all matters of tax policy and analysis as based on common sense are oversimplifying matters and either unaware of, or ignorant of, the complexities of tax policy. Of course, a widespread and supposedly "commonsense" idea of modern tax theory is that the wealthy should not pay taxes. That view often arises from application of religious views to tax policy, which are presented as "common sense." Yet these inspired views on tax policy are often thought to be common sense exactly because the person with a religiously inspired view thinks it is incontrovertible and is therefore not able to objectively evaluate it. Accordingly, because tax policy is a complex subject matter, science or scientific methods, not common-sense or tradition, are a superior way to approach policy analysis on the topic of taxation.

Analytical economic papers often contain a section titled "Theory"—doesn't that mean those writers are using a valid epistemology that should be considered modern?

Answer: An analytical paper usually contains a section labeled "Theory" and another labeled "Model," and they are laid out to suggest that the Theory section gave rise to the Model section of the respective paper. The implication, then, is that some aspect of the theory is being tested by the model presented. This is not really the case. In a scientific paper, the "Theory" section would actually describe the theory of causation that the writer of the paper will go on to test. Usually in economic papers the "model" is instead formulated independently from the theory, and the "Theory" section is simply just a review of the existing literature. Econometric scholars then go on to identify patterns in a data set and infer causation from the patterns and then just toss in a "theory" later. This approach does not reflect the testing of a hypothesis, however, as the methodology represents only the identification of patterns without the prior statement of a causal theory.

Is moral philosophy a valid theory of knowing things about taxation?

Answer: Moral philosophy is a valid way of knowing, but it is a premodern way of knowing and thus unlikely to be persuasive to persons that do not share the underlying moral beliefs. For example, workers are not likely to agree they should pay taxes simply because they are the "little people." This disagreement will exist even if it is entirely cogent for Leona Helmsley to believe that workers are "little" and therefore ought to pay the taxes in society. Moral philosophy is designed to determine what is right and wrong, or good and bad, from a particular perspective, and is not intended as a description of cause and effect. Furthermore, different moral philosophies reach different results about right and wrong typically by varying what counts as a consequence in making the determination of right and wrong.

Accordingly, moral philosophy can never be Modern in the philosophical sense. For example, moral philosophy does not bear at all on the question of whether tax cuts for large corporations cause economic growth; rather, it says that such tax cuts are right or "fair" without even beginning to explain the why of how tax cuts might be thought to cause economic growth.

Karl Popper and other philosophers of science wanted to move forward and away from this moral theorizing to incorporate the testing of causal theory by evidence. Notably, because Modern science allows for the adjustment of beliefs from evidence, a much more rapid advancement in the predictive quality of beliefs is possible. That is, instead of waiting 300 years for a monk with the skills and social standing necessary to adjust the accepted interpretation of a scroll, any person with access to evidence could attempt to disprove a causal theory. And, it turns out that human understanding advances much more quickly with that latter version of scientific inquiry in comparison to moral philosophy. This is why Popper's book was entitled The Origins of Scientific *Discovery*. The word "discovery" in the title implies a more rapid advancement of scientific knowledge. It also entails the mere possibility of updates to scientific beliefs as Popper also dealt with the possible validity of methods that do not allow for any new ideas or discovery.

Scientific methods seem to allow for discovery where an unexpected theory of causation can be proposed and defended by scholars, such as Einstein's theory of relativity. Is it possible to reach this type discovery using economic methods?

Answer: No. Economic methods generally do not allow for discovery via unexpected results. For example, if Einstein had attempted to publish the theory of relativity under today's review standards for economic journals, it probably never would have been published. This is because the results of Einstein's theory were not always consistent with Newtonian theory. In a parallel fashion, under current economic methods of analysis, even if taxes on labor were inefficient to the economy, any economic study that concludes as much is unlikely to be published. This is because economists have nearly unlimited discretion in choosing the analytical models they will apply; accordingly, any analytical models that do not reach conclusions that are consistent with standard economic thought or expectations, or do not advance the moral precepts of economic theory, are simply never published. In this way, the publication today of ideas on taxation and tax policy works much like a medieval scribe who just carefully copies down scrolls for future generations without making any new interpretation and having no room for innovation. In other words, in economics, as in a monastery, there is little or no room for discovery and the methods are not at all scientific.

Do economic ideas about taxation and tax policy ever change?

Answer: Not really. Current economic methods generally do not allow for changes to standard economic doctrine. This is essentially the problem Popper identified of an epistemology that does not allow for advancement in the form of the incorporation or any new ideas. Economic analysis seems likely to go on with the conclusion that taxes should always be levied on workers and never the wealthy forward indefinitely into the future unless and until tax scholars begin to object on the grounds that economics as applied to tax policy does not yield accurate predictions of results.

Are economic ideas about taxation subject to falsification by testing with data or evidence?

Answer: No. A few scholars have even suggested that no economic model has ever been abandoned because of falsification by testing as would be the scientific approach.[7] The possibility of falsification was identified by Popper as the hallmark of a proper scientific theory. For example, the existence of ghosts in a creaky house is the classic example of an existential claim that is not a hypothesis that is subject to falsification by observation or experimentation. Falsification generally means the use of observation or experimentation to disprove a hypothesis; the potential to disprove must be at least possible. The exclusion of these sort of inconsistent observations occurs because economic methods as applied to taxation generally do not include testing by the gathering of data or evidence, as would otherwise be required in science or by the scientific method. Even so, economic analysis is often apparently falsified accidentally by and through human experience with actual economic events. That is, evidence pops up from time to time that strongly indicates that an economic claim may not be accurate. For example, after the passage of the tax reform in 2017, including arguably the largest corporate tax cut in human history, there has been no observed decrease at all in consumer prices. If it were true that corporate tax cuts result in consumer price reductions, we would expect to see that after the largest corporate tax cut in history, and we do not. That sort of inconsistent data is a serious problem in science but not in economics.

The concept of falsification in the philosophy of science can be explained in another way. The idea that corporate tax cuts cause economic growth is presumed to be true based on theory. No evidence is thought by economists to be necessary in support of this hypothesis. For comparison, for centuries, every scientist knew the earth was flat and simply ignored countervailing evidence. Similarly, in economics, any countervailing results that seem to falsify some aspect of an economic theory can be incorporated by updating the simplified model. For example, one might simply update Laffer's existential claim of a U-shaped function of tax collections to say that the reason the theory has yet to ever yield an accurate result in practice is that we are on the upward and not on the downward sloping side of the U-shaped function. Given the belief in the presumptive validity of economic theory, such as the Laffer curve, it is extremely difficult to ever change an economist's mind about anything, even with contrary evidence. Likewise, this was also true with respect of the methodology of science in other fields of study during the century when economics was borne in the period roughly from 1676 to 1776.

Each economist I see on television seems to have a different view on tax policy—aren't there too many hypotheses in economics as opposed to too few?

Answer: Yes, this is indeed true. The lack of testing in the discipline of economics means that each individual economist is likely to make idiosyncratic predictions about tax policy or other matters of economic policy. And because there are tens of thousands of economists making these idiosyncratic predictions, we have tens of thousands of predictions about tax policy. None of these predictions about tax policy is likely ever tested, and therefore, none is ever shown to be wrong. Yet, nearly all of the thousands of predictions of economic theory about taxes are implausible because most of economic theory does not relate to the real world. The pool of predictions has continued to grow almost indefinitely, so there are economic "theories" in support of nearly every possible hypothesis relating to tax.

An unlimited explosion of idiosyncratic ideas about tax policy is strong evidence—proof, really—that the given methodology of economics is not science. Professional science involves the screening of hypothesis that the scientist either already knows to be false, or which he or she may find to be unlikely, and therefore without merit for further scientific testing. Professional scientists are engaged in this "screening" process on a regular basis, essentially sorting out ideas using their expertise. In comparison to professional scientists, laypersons have a difficult time sorting ideas about tax policy into ideas that are probably true and worthy of testing and those that are probably not true and should be abandoned. Notably, this is true not just with respect to taxation but also with respect to any other topic of science to which laypersons are involved but lack training or knowledge. So, as a layperson views any subject matter, including as the prime example taxation or tax policy, there are a great pool of possibilities that might be true in relation to tax policy. For example, a layperson might be unsure if the earth is flat or the earth is round—either *could be true* in the absence of scientific training. If a layperson claims the earth is flat that really just indicates not a lack of intelligence, rather an unfamiliarity with scientific developments over the past 400 years. The hypothesis that the earth is round has survived a vastly greater degree of scientific testing and review. The foregoing explains why professional scientists often are aggravated, or appear to be aggravated, when they are contacted by laypersons who have a keen interest in the field of study and wish to propose a hypothesis. The professional scientist may view this as a waste of time because the process of becoming a scientist means that person has become an "expert" in that particular area by familiarizing herself with all that has been done by others previously in that field. In scientific terms, an "expert" is a person who knows that is *not* true by studying the hypotheses previously proposed in that field and is able to quickly sort through causal hypotheses.

In summary, within the discipline of economics, hypotheses are essentially never tested and eliminated. It remains possible to argue about competing hypothesis, but these arguments are never resolved in a scientific way. The scientific means to resolve an argument is for someone to devise a test. That also means that when tax professionals (i.e., clinicians) encounter economic predictions about taxation and tax policy in academic settings, the tax professionals will often become frustrated or, commonly get up and walk out of economic presentations, because the tax professional knows the prediction or idea presented by the economist is false or implausible for some reason. That type of professional skepticism is what it means to be a "professional" in taxation or anything else where implausible ideas are screened out. The occasionally obnoxious process that often occurs at scholarly conferences where a person stands up and asks a series of questions to the speaker is a healthy process and characterizes scientific inquiry. The problem is further aggravated insofar as the field of economics has grafted itself onto many other disciplines, from tax to nearly all other areas of social science. The bottom line is that economists have ideas about everything but are essentially "experts" in nothing including tax policy to which they have little or no clinical knowledge or expertise.

Isn't it obvious to others, including tax policymakers, that economic models don't yield accurate results on tax policy?

Answer: Yes, absolutely. Various US presidents—notably Harry Truman—have even become angry with their economic advisors.[8] Likewise, academic papers are written all the time that show that economic models are flawed because they cannot be used to formulate reliable economic predictions. For example, modern tax policy is based on *tax incidence* analysis, in which labor is thought to always bear the "incidence" of taxes even if those taxes are ostensibly paid by "capital," meaning large corporations.[9] Experienced tax professionals have pointed out to economists that this makes little sense because large corporations behave as if they bear the incidence of corporate tax.[10] That is, everyone ought to know that large corporations engage in very aggressive tax avoidance and hire thousands of tax accountants and lawyers toward this end. Professional tax advisors and other scholars have pretty clearly explained and illustrated by example that the economic theory of tax incidence makes no sense, but economists continue to apply the theory of tax incidence like gospel. In other words, economists have continued to use tax incidence analysis even after this so-called model has been roundly rebuked. The tax incidence model, together with the Laffer curve, represents the most overwhelming flaw in the use of nonscientific methods of analysis in economics.

The neoclassical economic idea of "tax incidence" was developed by Arnold Harberger, who called it the small open-economy model, and is now incorporated into the theory of international tax competition.[11] Harberger created two parallel models, one open-economy model, one closed-economy model. The US economy is open and large. Economists nonetheless premise their US tax policy on the closed model. This approach is odd because within the model, the policy conclusions reverse each time the conditions of the model are adjusted. In science, a theorist cannot simultaneously advocate two opposing models as a causal explanation, which is what the tax incidence model does. Thus, even preeminent economists have been known to admit that they choose the model simply because they like the policy results reflecting a nonscientific methodology. Harberger's model has been further developed into the theory of corporate tax competition giving rise to what is often thought to be a "race to the bottom" in international tax policy.

Are there any other illustrations of nonscience in economic methods of tax research?

Answer: Yes. Another illustration of the lack of a scientific epistemology in economics is the discussion of "death taxes," the term commonly used to refer to estate and inheritance taxes. The federal estate exemption amount was raised to over $11 million, so the estate tax applies only to extremely wealthy individuals. Various tax scholars have objected to these kinds of taxes on the basis of various types of moral philosophy, such as libertarianism, which reflects a premodern approach. So, what should we expect economic theory premised on efficiency to say about death taxes? First, we would expect to find a discussion of the relative efficiency of these types of taxes compared to other tax types. The economic theory of tax incidence suggests that taxes should be levied on the immobile factor of production. Because capital is considered mobile, and labor, immobile, then labor should pay all the tax. Applying the same analysis, we could expect that inheritances and estates would be ideal for levying tax, right? Dead people are not very mobile; in fact, dead people are even less mobile than workers. Yet what does the economic analysis say about death taxes? Why, they are bad, very bad, of course! The inability to apply Harberger's ideal of the respective mobility of the factors of production to other fields of taxation, such as estate and gift taxation where it ought to apply, suggests that the idea is also invalid as it is traditionally applied in international taxation.

But, even the methodology of modern science has been challenged in many ways, right? Are we still able to use science or the scientific method in tax given that it has been challenged by later philosophers?

Answer: Yes. The philosophy of science has continued to evolve since the early twentieth century. Popper was perhaps the leading philosopher of science and much of what has followed him is premised on his initial work. However, some critiques have been levied against Popper's theory. A leading critique is that not many theories are ever subject to outright falsification, and many are instead augmented with incremental ideas. In addition, Bayesian science has evolved as another standard of science, wherein scientific ideas are sometimes determined by consensus among scientists—and economists have been known to do things this way.[12] The consensus view is then taken to be the scientific view. However, this approach is flawed where it is applied without any testing of economic ideas. A consensus view of any matter of science would only be valid in the interpretation of testing results, perhaps where conflicting test results had been obtained and scientists disagreed then on whether a theory was in need of revision. A poll of economists on matters for which no data or evidence has been obtained or will ever be obtained is meaningless. That consensus-type approach is really no different than polling a group of monks on the accepted meaning of a scroll held in a monastery.

What do you mean by the term postmodern? Is Postmodern thought relevant to taxation and tax policy?

Answer: Postmodern thought is essentially a formal philosophical challenge to Modernism or the validity of prior epistemology, here as applied to taxation and tax policy. Postmodernism arose in the second half of the twentieth century. Basically, Postmodern ideas critique any epistemology or method of knowing usually on the grounds that society reflects power relations and not efficiency ideals. The famous postmodern philosopher Richard Rorty levied perhaps the most effective philosophical critique of epistemology.[13] In order to make taxation and tax policy Modern—that is, to bring it into the twentieth century—any resulting epistemology would basically need to be able to withstand a Postmodern critique. One response to Rorty's postmodern critique of Modernist thought generally was given by Jürgen Habermas, who said that there are certain universals in human experience that could form an epistemology in some particular cases—and tax collection might be one of those cases.[14]

CONCLUSION ON THE EPISTEMOLOGY OF TAXATION

An additional question remains as part of this inquiry into the nature of scientific inquiry and tax policy: How can we undertake scientific methods in tax research? The answer is that the study of taxation is a category of social science. It is therefore premised on understanding human behavior. Persons with "clinical" knowledge of taxation about the behavior of taxpayers, including the tax laws that are generally presumed to drive human behavior, would be ideal to formulate hypotheses and causal theories on taxation and tax policy. Economists would be more suited to testing theories of causation likely developed by these clinicians. What would tax discourse look like, though, if tax practitioners were in charge? First, nearly all tax practitioners would agree that large corporations engage in tax avoidance, suggesting that capital bears the incidence of taxation including both capital and labor taxation. Second, tax practitioners usually set out to defer the levy of tax on their clients. Experienced tax advisors should universally agree that the availability of tax deferral is a key aspect of tax policy design. Because tax deferral is only available to capital, and rarely to labor, this suggests that the tax system is favorable to capital irrespective of the progressivity of the rate structure. Finally, tax practitioners often work to maximize the value of tax deductions, especially to their business clients of capital investment. This would suggest that higher tax rates would increase the value of deductions arising from capital reinvestment from firms that are already profitable in the jurisdiction. Therefore, capital investment could be expected to flow into higher-tax jurisdictions rather than tax havens, as occurs in the actual world, where capital continues to flow into higher-tax jurisdictions such as Japan, South Korea, the United Kingdom, Germany, the United States and so on.

NOTES

1 Karl Popper, *The Logic of Scientific Discovery*, 2nd edn. (London: Routledge; Classics: New York, 2002), at 94.
2 Kenneth Feder, *Frauds, Myths, and Mysteries, Science and Pseudoscience in Archaeology*, 5th edn. (New York: McGraw Hill, 2001), at 32.
3 Richard G. Anderson & William G. Dewald, *Replication and Scientific Standards in Applied Economics a Decade After the Journal of Money, Credit and Banking Project*, 76:6 Fed. R. Bank St. Louis Rev. 79, 81 (1994).
4 Popper, *The Logic of Scientific Discovery*, at 90 ("[T]he theoretician must long before [experimentation] have done his work, or at least what is the most important part of his work: he must have formulated his question as sharply as possible. Thus it is he who shows the experimenter the way. But even the experimenter is not in the main engaged in making exact observations; his work, too, is largely of a theoretical kind. Theory dominates the experimental work from its initial planning up to the finishing touches in the laboratory.").
5 Popper, *The Logic of Scientific Discovery*, at 9.
6 Bret N. Bogenschneider, *Causation, Science & Taxation*, 10 Elon L. Rev. 1 (2017).
7 Donald N. McCloskey, *The Rhetoric of Economics*, 21 J. Econ. Lit. 481, 482 (1983); Aris Spanos, *Statistical Foundations of Econometric Modelling* (Cambridge: Cambridge University Press, 1986), at 660.
8 Herbert Stein, How to Introduce an Economist, in *On the Third Hand: Humor in the Dismal Science, an Anthology*, ed. Clotfelter, 5 (Ann Arbor: University of Michigan Press, 1996) ("As President Truman said, 'I wish that I had a one-armed economist, so that he wouldn't say on the one hand and on the other hand.'").
9 See Arnold C. Harberger, Efficiency Effects of Taxes on Income from Capital, in *Effects of Corporation Income Tax*, ed. Marian Krzyzaniak, 107, 114–17 (Detroit, MI: Wayne State University Press, 1966); Arnold C. Harberger, Taxation, Resource Allocation and Welfare, in *The Role of Direct and Indirect Taxes in the Federal Reserve System* 25, 42–52 (1964), http://www.nber.org/chapters/c1873.pdf. Accessed Nov. 10, 2019.
10 See Clausing, *In Search of Corporate Tax Incidence*, 65 Tax L. Rev. 433, 438–45 (2012).

11 See Michael Keen & Kai Konrad, The Theory of International Tax Competition and Coordination, in *Handbook of Public Economics*, ed. Alan Auerbach, Raj Chetty, Martin Feldstein & Emmanuel Saez, volume 5 (Amsterdam: Elsevier B.V., 2013).

12 See N. Gregory Mankiw, *Smart Taxes: An Open Invitation to Join the Pigou Club*, 35 EASTERN ECON. J. 14–23 (2009).

13 Richard Rorty, *Philosophy and the Mirror of Nature* (Princeton, NJ: Princeton University Press, 1979).

14 Jürgen Habermas, Richard Rorty's Pragmatic Turn, in *Rorty and His Critics* 31, 49 (Malden, MA: Blackwell, 2000); Bret N. Bogenschneider, *A Philosophy Toolkit for Tax Lawyers*, 3:3 AKRON L. REV. 50 (2017).

CHAPTER 3

HOW THE BUSINESS TAX SYSTEM FAVORS LARGE CORPORATIONS OVER SMALL BUSINESSES

Chapter Summary: *Small businesses did not benefit very much from the Tax Cuts and Jobs Act of 2017 since very few small businesses will qualify for the new 20 percent pass-through deduction. The result is that large corporations enjoy extremely low tax rates in comparison to small businesses and thereby have an extraordinary competitive advantage in the marketplace. This tax system is not "neutral" and heavily favors big business over small business. The primary source of the advantage to large firms is "transfer pricing," which refers to the internal sale of products between divisions of the same company. In addition, small business owners are subject to double taxation on earnings more so than large corporations. Because of the double tax on wage earnings, the applicable tax rate for small business owners is actually higher than the statutory income tax rate. The widely reported "corporate inversion" scare leading up to the passage of the tax cuts was a scare tactic and deception designed to mislead voters. In fact, there was no prospect of job losses or an erosion of the tax base as a result of corporate inversions. The tax concept of corporate tax competition is also a deception; investment capital actually flows into higher-tax jurisdictions, and not into tax havens, because multinational firms are generally able to harvest the tax deductions that result from capital investment such as depreciation on business assets and to shift any profits out of the tax net using transfer-pricing techniques.*

One of the more significant events in modern political history occurred with the last-minute amendments to the Tax Cuts and Jobs Act of 2017. These amendments related to changes in the tax treatment of small business. Of course, the primary objective of the overall tax reform was to cut the corporate tax rates for big business, not small business. The focus on the tax treatment of large corporations as opposed to other categories of taxpayers should come as no surprise because most of the lobbyists in Washington work for large corporations. But at the last minute, tax cuts for small business were also added into the tax reform, as proposed by House leaders including former Speaker of the House Paul Ryan. These took the form of a special 20 percent deduction for qualifying businesses. Unfortunately, as this chapter explains, it is unclear whether many small businesses will qualify for this new 20 percent tax deduction.[1] Eligibility will be based on tax regulations that were released by the Internal Revenue Service (IRS) in final form only as of January 2019. Tax practitioners are thus still figuring out which small businesses may qualify, but most tax practitioners think that very few small businesses, apart from real estate companies, may qualify for the new 20 percent tax deduction.

Of course, the tax cuts for big business were understood as the primary objective of the whole process, and Congress had already agreed, with the necessary votes at the final stage of debate over the bill. Therefore, it was, to say the least, problematic to introduce late-stage amendments to reduce small business taxes at the very end of the political debate over business tax reform. The discussion of small business taxation so late in the game was difficult for the congressional leadership because of how tax bills are scored. The term "scored" refers to the process of budgeting or estimating how much a tax provision will cost. The tax cuts for small business made it more difficult to "score" the tax reform bill in a way that would make it possible to pass, and as explained in the following paragraphs, this is partly why the corporate tax rate was reduced only to 21 percent, and not 20 percent, as had initially been proposed.[2]

CONGRESSIONAL BUDGET OFFICE SCORING OF TAX REFORM PROPOSALS

The term "scored" refers to the way Congress determines how much revenue (or cost) to assign to each tax provision in a piece of legislation. If an item is scored to have a relatively high budgetary cost, then it is more difficult to include it in a bill because each tax bill must be revenue neutral over 10 years. For this reason, the Congressional Budget Office (CBO) and its scoring process for legislative proposals are critical to the political debates in Congress. During the debate over a bill, the CBO sets out to create a dollar estimate of the change to the federal budget—that is, how much the item costs—that is associated with each particular item included in the legislation. This is because there is a federal law on the books that says budgetary items must be revenue neutral over 10 years.[3]

The CBO's scoring largely determines whether the items comply with that requirement of federal law. Whether the scoring turns out to be accurate taken in retrospect is not important; the only federal requirement is that the CBO estimate each bill to be revenue neutral over 10 years. Rather obviously (at least from the perspective of tax experts familiar with background data on the relation between tax rates and tax collections) a tax increase is generally scored to have a revenue benefit, whereas a tax cut is scored to have a revenue detriment. In other words, the predictions of the Laffer curve where tax cuts are posited to result in greater tax receipts have not been accepted as methodology at the CBO. Some debate continues today about whether the tax cuts should be scored as a revenue cost, meaning that less revenue would be collected at the lower rate, or as a revenue benefit, meaning that more revenue would be collected at the lower rate (following the reasoning of the Laffer curve). The CBO staffers have thus far refused to follow the Laffer curve, given their prior experience in tax cuts that did not generate any incremental revenue. However, the political pressure on the staffers at that government office to apply the Laffer curve to justify tax cuts must be tremendous.

In the actual political process of forming tax policy, the underlying economic theory is important because it determines the scoring methodology. Economic theory prescribes essentially how the CBO will calculate the score. For example, in the scoring for the Tax Cuts and Jobs Act of 2017, the budgetary cost of tax cuts for big business was scored relatively lightly, reflecting "macroeconomic feedback" effects of the tax cuts.[4] In other words, it was assumed that the tax cuts granted to big business would be reinvested into the economy, thereby creating economic growth and eventual increases in tax revenue. The tax cuts for small business were then added in with a lesser "macroeconomic feedback" amount. Interestingly, every government has a different terminology for the extraordinary benefits of tax cuts toward creating economic growth. For example, in the United Kingdom, this is called "dynamic effects"; in the United States, it is called "macroeconomic feedback" effects. Whatever you call it, though, there is no empirical evidence that these effects actually exist in the world. This is to say, the economic theory used to score congressional bills is not performed in a scientific manner premised on the respective evidence.

Because of the legal requirement of deficit neutrality over 10 years, and given the last-minute inclusion of the small business tax items in the most recent tax reform bill, adjustments needed to be incorporated for other budgetary items, in order to offset the added cost to the federal budget over ten years. These adjustments are referred to as "offsets." Offsets often reduce the budget implications of a tax cut through a tax increase for someone else; or in the tax reform of 2017, tax cuts for small business meant lower tax cuts for someone else. The scoring of the tax cuts for small business made it less likely that the tax cuts for big business would be considered revenue neutral over ten years and, therefore, eligible to be voted on by Congress under federal law.

The tax reform bill in its final form thereby incorporated offsets in the form of tax increases on other persons in the United States (mostly in so-called blue states) by removing tax preferences, such as the deduction for state and local taxes (referred to by the acronym "SALT"). The elimination of this deduction was added in to the legislation to act as an offset against the cost of the small business tax cuts not based on evidence. The corporate tax rate was also lowered to 21 percent, as opposed to the originally proposed 20 percent. One problem is that the CBO's scoring method relies on the economic theory of macroeconomic feedback effects of tax cuts. Hence, the estimates of the likely 10-year effects of each item included in the Tax Cuts and Jobs Act of 2017 were likely to be wrong largely because the theory applied to create the estimates is implausible. The theory used to do the scoring has never been tested in the real world using data or evidence. Nevertheless, it was the "scoring" of each tax item that led the tax reform bill to include the unpopular SALT provisions, which have caused so much hardship to persons living in states with high property taxes, such as New Jersey, Illinois, New Hampshire and Wisconsin.

ON THE SO-CALLED DOUBLE TAXATION OF LARGE CORPORATIONS

The tax issues within the Tax Cuts and Jobs Act of 2017 were both debated and scored by Congress largely using the nomenclature of "pass-through" versus "double taxation." The term "pass through" describes the taxation of small businesses that are not incorporated (as a C corporation for tax purposes). As seemingly every politician, television and radio commentator wishes us to know, if a business is incorporated, it potentially faces corporate tax and also shareholder tax if it pays out cash dividends. These two levels of tax are referred to colloquially as "double taxation." Of course, this term is ideological more than anything, as it makes little sense to speak in terms of double taxation for many reasons. This will be explained further in this section.

Large corporations remit only a tiny amount of tax relative to their profits, and shareholders, even less. The tax revenues from capital gains are so small that the Internal Revenue Service generally does not release the historical data on them to the public (except during times of high stock market gains). In practical terms, this means that the tax system is so unfair to working taxpayers that the government will not publicly release statistics about tax collection when the results are not favorable, because if it did, the result would be popular unrest, maybe even riots. Again, there is nothing smart, fair, or efficient about the tax system.

The "double taxation" terminology of corporate taxation is designed to deceive us about who actually pays taxes into the system. For as long as I can remember, the so-called tax policy experts have proposed that large corporations are potentially subject to two layers of tax. However, there has been no attempt to determine whether these supposed two layers add up to more than the one layer of tax that small businesses pay. If double taxation were really a valid method for understanding tax policy, then the foremost example of it in the modern tax system would be the taxation of wage income, not corporate taxes. Labor earnings are taxed under the Social Security system by withholding from the worker's paycheck and then taxed again under the income tax system, including the portion of wage earnings never received by the worker. This is certainly double taxation—and it effects nearly everyone who works. If the worker ultimately collects Social Security benefits, those amounts may be subject to tax a third time upon receipt depending on the circumstances, including the income level of the recipient when the Social Security benefits are received.

ILLUSTRATION OF THE DOUBLE TAXATION OF SMALL BUSINESS OWNERS AND SOLE PROPRIETORS

Small business owners are subject to self-employment taxation, meaning that they must pay both the employee and employer portion of Social Security taxes plus Medicare taxes. A deduction from income tax is available for only 50 percent of the amount paid for those taxes, reflecting the employer portion of the wage taxes. Thus, as is true of all workers, whether self-employed or not, small business owners pay double tax on the portion of wage tax withholding that does not create an income tax deduction. Here, "double tax" refers not to the two types of tax, but rather to double levy of tax on the same income. This can be illustrated (using rounded whole numbers, for simplicity's sake) as follows:

Step 1: Withholding of Wage Taxes from Wages

Owner Salary or Wages	$50,000
Employee Part of Wage Taxes	($5,000)
Net Receipts	$45,000

Query: *How much "taxable income" does the worker or small business owner receive for purposes of income taxation: $50,000 or $45,000?* Answer: $50,000.

Therefore, if the statutory federal and state income tax rate on the worker is 40 percent, that figure is not the final tax rate, which must be higher because the statutory tax rate is assessed on the gross amount of worker wages, not net receipts; it can be calculated at 44.4 percent. In other words, the worker does not receive an income tax deduction for the employee portion of Social Security and Medicare taxes withheld from his or her paycheck.

Step 2: Levy of Income Tax on Gross Wages

Wages	$50,000
×40% Statutory Tax Rate	× 0.40
Income Taxes Payable	$20,000

Step 3: Calculation of Worker's Applicable Income Tax Rate

Net Receipts	$45,000
Income Taxes Payable	($20,000)

Therefore: $\dfrac{\$20,000}{\$45,000}$ = 44.4% applicable income tax rate (i.e., not the 40 percent statutory rate).

Step 4: Calculation of Small Business Owner's Effective Tax Rate after Both Wage and Income Tax

Owner Salary or Wages	$50,000
Wage Taxes Paid by Withholding	($5,000)
Income Taxes Paid	($20,000)

Therefore: $\dfrac{\$25,000}{\$50,000}$ = 50% effective tax rate

Notwithstanding that small business owners and other workers are subject to double taxation, and an untold, vast amount of taxes is collected from small business owners and workers by this unfair method, this methodology is where we really must begin, because the modern political discourse on taxation hinges on the concept of double taxation of *large corporations*. The ideology of double taxation of corporate profits suggests that pass-through taxation is more desirable for small businesses, and it is designed to imply that small business are treated more favorably under the tax system than corporations, especially large corporations, which are subject to corporate income tax as well as shareholder tax when they pay out dividends.

In broad terms, small businesses can elect to pay tax as a pass-through, which means they pay taxes instead at the individual tax rate (as an S corporation, partnership, or sole proprietorship) and thus avoid corporate tax. This leaves only a single level of tax levied at the owner level. Although it is true that pass-through entities pay only one level of tax, it does not constitute the pertinent point of tax policy for several reasons because other business forms also tend to pay only one level of tax as well. The primary reason for this is that large corporations tend to accumulate earnings within the corporation and not pay dividends, to avoid any second level of tax. Simply put, corporations can elect when to pay dividends or if they will pay dividends at all. Corporations can elect not to pay dividends to shareholders because the Internal Revenue Service does not enforce the accumulated earnings tax against large multinational corporations. The accumulated earnings tax is a special tax that was designed to cause corporations to pay out accumulated earnings as dividends to shareholders. That means that the shareholder level of tax can be deferred endlessly: as long as the large corporation does not pay any dividends, there is no second level of tax.

Any capital gains on shareholders' corporate stock would be taxed at the lower capital gains rate. Nonetheless, when a corporation does not elect to pay dividends, the market price of its stock could increase because the market would see the company as retaining profits, and that increase in stock value could create capital gains for shareholders. Those potential capital gains and resulting taxes at the shareholder level might also be considered a second layer of tax, notwithstanding the dividends were not paid and there was no tax on them. However, the capital gains tax is rarely discussed in these terms, since it so rarely applies.

There are at least three reasons the capital gains tax rarely applies and so raises so little revenue in practice. The first is what I call the "Warren Buffet method," or avoiding capital gains tax on holdings in corporate stock by never selling the stock. The capital gains tax applies only when stock is sold, and the stock sale triggers the gain, so large stock holdings are often held indefinitely as a means of tax deferral. If a large shareholder needs cash, it is entirely lawful to simply go to the bank and borrow with stock holdings serving as collateral. The act of borrowing is not taxable; neither the borrowing nor the repayment triggers a taxable event. The second reason capital gains tax rarely applies on stock holdings is that corporate shares are often held in nontaxable accounts (e.g., retirement 401(k)s or individual retirement accounts (IRAs) or similar accounts) or by nontaxable shareholders, such as pension funds. The third reason is that when investment funds hold large blocks of stock, if a stock is sold at a gain, savvy investors will match any gains against other losses and net the difference to zero for tax purposes. The idea is simply to hold the winners and sell the losers; if you have to sell a winner, then offset that gain against the loss on several others. A significant amount of capital gains tax in the investment community is avoided through this lawful strategy of matching gains and losses. Thus, even though large corporations that don't pay dividends retain cash and so create the potential for capital gains for shareholders, this is unlikely to apply very often as a practical matter. The very wealthy who own large blocks of corporate stock have simple means to avoid tax, including by simply holding the stock indefinitely and borrowing against it if a need for cash arises.

SMALL BUSINESSES VERSUS LARGE CORPORATIONS

Small businesses typically pay higher effective tax rates than multinational firms. The IRS does not release data with sufficient detail for us to calculate the rate applicable to small business taxpayers, but the differential in comparison to large corporations is so obvious to tax practitioners that a calculation is unnecessary (see the discussion on this below). The relevant tax statistic in the formation of tax policy is effective tax rate, not statutory tax rate or marginal tax rate. Because small business pay higher effective tax rates than large multinational corporations, this means that the tax system benefits large corporations and is not neutral. Tax policy is often intended to be neutral, though, meaning that it does not favor one taxpayer over another in similar factual situations. The non-neutrality of the business tax system means that in situations where, say, a local small business is in competition with a large multinational, the small business is at a disadvantage because of the tax system. As explained earlier, it appears that in the late-stage debate over the Tax Cuts and Jobs Act of 2017, some politicians from the Midwest (and other places with historically high concentrations of small businesses) may have realized that it could be harmful to economic competition to create a tax system where large multinationals pay almost no tax and small businesses pay tax at a high pass-through rate. In the lead up to the passage of the tax bill in 2017, I published a paper called "Small Business Tax Neutrality" identifying the pertinent issue of tax policy.[5] Ironically, at least one economist in the United States replied to that timely paper on tax policy and said that the concept of tax neutrality was not intended to relate to neutrality between small businesses and large corporations as a matter of economic theory, so I must have misunderstood. I got a good laugh out of that—small business tax neutrality is in actual fact one of the most important matters of tax policy of modern times.

To further explain why small business tax neutrality is important, it will be helpful to summarize the tax rates on small versus large firms. The *effective tax rate* of large multinational corporations that are engaged in the same particular line of business as a small business is often about one-tenth that of small business, even those operating with pass-through taxation. Consider a large multinational corporation that is engaged in a particular line of business, say, operating coffee shops, and has a 5 percent effective tax rate on profits. A good rule of thumb is that a small business engaged in operating coffee shops would typically have a 50 percent effective tax rate on any profits. I suspect that this one-tenth ratio of effective tax between small and large business is actually an informal rule that tax policymakers use in behind-the-scenes political negotiations on taxation. In any debate over tax policy, there must be a baseline ratio that political leaders or lobbyists have with one another in debating a bill on taxation, and that baseline is likely established by reference to what has been done previously. Any change to the tax system, then, is a deviation from the traditional baseline. So, it may be a matter of tradition that the baseline effective tax rate of small business is intentionally set at a rate that is ten times that of large business. In this case, congressional leaders would be aware of the baseline and use it as an informal rule for what might be considered a reasonable change to tax policy. A traditional baseline approach to tax policy of small businesses being required to pay ten times what large businesses do seems plausible because it would be so advantageous to those large corporations that compete with small business that the CEOs of large corporations would deem it acceptable to target the effective tax rate to that relative level of taxation. This is essentially the "big business can't lose" tradition in tax policy. Interestingly, there is no empirical evidence that a large corporation has ever actually gone out of business because of tax benefits being granted to small businesses it competes with. The tax system drastically and categorically favors large corporations in every possible and conceivable circumstance.

So, how could policymakers who are ostensibly interested in economic growth favor non-neutral taxation between small and big businesses in a tax system that already substantially favors large multinational corporations? Political lobbying—large corporations lobbying of elected representatives is significantly more advanced than the lobbying efforts of small business. Because of lobbying, the financial interests of large corporations prevail most of the time in the formulation of tax policy.

CORPORATE INVERSIONS: ARE COMPANIES REALLY LEAVING THE UNITED STATES?

I've been arguing so far in this book that nearly all of tax policy is a magic show. In any magic show, the magician directs and controls the audience's attention, and having this control is an essential part of whether the audience believes the magician's tricks. Consider the debate over corporate inversions leading up to the passage of the Tax Cuts and Jobs Act of 2017. A "corporate inversion" is a tax-motivated business reorganization in which a firm controlled by US shareholders is sold offshore and the control of that firm shifts to foreign shareholders. Hundreds of magazine and newspaper articles, as well as academic journal papers, were published on how harmful corporate inversions are to the economy.[6] In this case, the magicians—politicians and tax policymakers— were hoping to set the stage for a reduction in the corporate tax rate, so they redirected the audience's attention to this idea of corporate tax and the "risk" of corporate inversion.

For example, the fast-food restaurant chain Burger King was "inverted" to become controlled by a Canadian company, Tim Hortons.[7] Burger King still operates outlets in the United States, even though it is now Canadian-owned. However, it is unlikely that many jobs or other business activities were largely affected by this shift in ownership. There was little or no practical effect on the operations of the Burger King restaurants operating across the United States, and everyone can still get a Whopper. Rather, in a corporate inversion, all the business operations of the US company stay the same and only the shareholder control shifts offshore. Really, the shifting of this shareholder control to Canada was relevant only to the company's calculation of tax in the United States. So, neither the tax base of Burger King nor its restaurant footprint was shifted from one country to another by the inversion transaction. The impact on US taxation of Burger King is also mundane contrary to what you have been led to believe. Profits from US restaurants are still fully taxable in the United States, and there were only some tax benefits from interest expense allocation and other technical rules, but not a full avoidance of tax where somehow a disgruntled Burger King had packed up shop and left the country. That simply did not happen. Anyone who has ever worked in corporate tax knows that large corporations often restructure or reorganize and the discussion over corporate inversions was intended to mislead the general public about corporate tax.

With this, corporate inversions became the feature of most news reports on tax policy before the Tax Cuts and Jobs Act of 2017.[8] The nonsensical premise of the reports is that when a US corporation inverts, it is terrible for the economy because the business shifts offshore—the implication made, though, is that jobs go offshore *and* the United States loses the ability to tax the company. The corporation is proposed to choose to pack up and leave because of supposedly high corporate tax rates. Corporate inversions are thus presented as proof that if any taxes are levied on the wealthy or large corporations, these folks will just pack up and leave—and when they do, that must be terrible because the wealthy and large corporations are the source of jobs, so let's not tax large corporations. Yet, this just isn't true. The United States has not lost jobs to corporate inversion. Likewise, the corporations that did "invert" did not do so because of high corporate tax in the United States but because of a lack of ideas among the senior executives for further business investment that is likely to generate a profit. And, reducing the corporate tax rate as a supposed policy solution to prevent corporate inversion—an imaginary problem in the first place—is also nonsense.

TECHNICAL EXPLANATION OF THE INTERNATIONAL TAX SYSTEM AS APPLICABLE TO MULTINATIONAL FIRMS

What follows is a technical explanation of how the system of international tax worked before the 2017 tax reforms. Feel free to skip to the next section if the details are not of interest to you.

So, this section explains the details of how international tax works in practice. The significance of a company's inversion for tax purposes is as follows. First, the company to be inverted (e.g., Burger King) may have significant stockpiles of cash sitting offshore in a variety of subsidiaries. If this cash were "repatriated" to the United States, it would trigger a tax equal to the difference between the tax rate in the foreign country where the funds are located (e.g., 20 percent) and the corporate tax rate in the United States, which under prior law, was 35 percent. That makes for a 15 percent difference in tax rates. The tax on repatriated profits occurs because the foreign profits were not taxed as the profits were earned. So, the profits just build up offshore until the cash returns to the United States. This delay of levied tax is known as deferral of taxation by tax accountants and lawyers. And deferral of taxation is the bread and butter of tax-planning activity, as it is what most tax accountants and lawyers try to achieve for their clients.

To return to the Burger King example, let's assume that there is a Burger King in a subway station in Vienna, Austria, and let's also assume that Austria has a tax rate of 20 percent. This means that as the restaurant sold Whoppers, fries and sodas to customers over the years, it paid 20 percent on its profits each year to the Austrian tax authorities. During that same time, it paid *no* corporate tax in the

United States on these same foreign profits. Prior to 2017, companies paid some tax on foreign profits only when the parent company, Burger King headquarters, so to speak, wanted to bring that cash back to the United States—for example, to pay dividends to its shareholders or to reduce its parent-level debt. At that point of "repatriation," Burger King pays tax on the difference between the Austrian tax rate already paid (20 percent) and the US corporate rate (35 percent, pre-2017), which means that it pays a 15 percent corporate tax rate. If Burger King had earned that money in the United States, it would have paid the 35 percent tax up front, so by delaying the payment of that tax, it is an advantage to the company. When it repatriates its profits, the company is just playing catch-up. Every multinational corporation is required to carefully track the amount of profits and the foreign taxes paid on those profits in special accounts referred to as earnings and profits accounts, or what tax experts call E&P.[9]

It is very important to note that, before the 2017 tax reforms in the United States, if the Burger King restaurant in our example were located instead in the Bahamas, which has a 0 percent tax rate, compared to Vienna's 20 percent, then Burger King would have paid $0 in corporate taxes in the Bahamas. If Burger King then wanted to repatriate those profits from the Bahamas back to the United States, it would be required to pay a residual tax of 35 percent, or the full corporate tax rate. Before 2017, multinational corporations generally did not want to pay tax at that rate, so the profits related to the Burger King in the Bahamas just sat there accumulating in the Bahamas. Those accumulating profits are the first objective of a corporate inversion. That is, if the Burger King parent company shifts offshore, it has no need to bring that pile of profits back to the United States at all. Instead, in the Burger King case, it can simply transfer the profits to Canada, which does not levy a tax on repatriated foreign profits. Then in Canada the Burger King company will choose to pay down debt or pay a dividend to shareholders or use the profits in some other way without having to pay US tax. Burger King, then, will never pay the residual tax—the difference between the tax it paid in the foreign country and the tax in the United States—because of its inversion.

But you might be wondering, if the Burger King parent company moves to Canada, doesn't that mean that the company is no longer subject to US corporate tax? No! Even after a so-called corporate inversion, the corporate profits that originate in the United States from the Burger King franchises operating inside the United States are still subject to the US corporate tax. Once Burger King became a Canadian company, it would be considered a foreign corporation, and the profits of foreign corporations that operate restaurants, or any other business, in the United States are still taxable!

The deceptions presented about corporate inversion in the news and media were rampant. First, was the implication that Burger King restaurants would close as a result of the inversion, and so jobs would be lost. This is false. An inversion does not change underlying business operations or shift jobs out of the United States. Second was the implication that any profits that Burger King made at the US locations would not be subject to US tax going forward. Also false. Foreign companies still pay corporate tax in the United States. Third was the suggestion that multinationals should be able to accumulate foreign profits without any limits and that the accumulated earnings tax never apply. False again! The IRS could have largely eliminated instances of corporate inversion simply by choosing to enforce the tax laws (including § 531, et seq.) against large corporations, not just small businesses. In that case, Burger King, as an example, would likely have been required to pay tax on its large stockpile of accumulated offshore earnings long ago. Thus, the push toward expatriation would have been eliminated as there would have been no stockpile of untaxed earnings waiting to be shifted into Canada with the takeover by Tim Hortons.

So, what are the actual tax-related objectives and results of corporate inversion? First and foremost, a corporate inversion eliminates the need to repatriate foreign profits back to the US parent corporation, which then avoids the levy of US corporate tax on foreign profits, not domestic profits. Notably, the Tax Cuts and Jobs Act of 2017 also eliminated future taxes on foreign profits. Logically speaking, then, if corporate inversions were a tax problem because of their potential to reduce US tax collections—as the magicians led us to believe—then that tax reform gave the same or similar tax benefits to all US multinationals from the reduction in tax rate, whether or not they inverted. Remember that the issue of multinational firms that were not paying US taxes on their accumulated foreign profits was first identified as the problem in need of a solution. The magicians' solution to that problem was to not tax those foreign profits at all. Yet, this was a poorly executed magic trick as polling data revealed the audience did not believe it as the polls indicated a lack of popular support for the tax reform. Everyone who favored the tax reform was silently confused by the tax discourse yet just kept clapping without really knowing what was going on in the hopes their 401(k) balance might increase.

Another actual result of corporate inversion is that the inversion transaction eliminated a special disallowance of interest deductions (from the ratio of foreign profits to US profits). In this situation, a highly leveraged company could increase the amount of allowable interest deductions in order to reduce the US tax it owes. However, this problem could have been easily fixed with a change to the US Treasury regulations as issued by the Internal Revenue Service. This topic was not a big deal to the Treasury, and certainly not a tax issue that warranted the attention of all Americans—all it did was scare everyone into believing that corporate inversions were a big deal and all of our jobs would flee to China, and so on.

So, now that you understand these technical aspects of corporate inversion transactions, a few questions arise:

How common were corporate inversions before 2017? If there was only a small tax benefit, if enough US multinationals inverted to take advantage of that, it could still be a problem in the aggregate, right?

Answer: Corporate inversions were not common at all. In the years leading up to the 2017 tax reform, any inversion was advertised and made into a big deal. Even Wall Street got into the action, pushing for tax reform by tracking inversions and inflating their effects on the US economy. However, the US economy is quite large—there are thousands of multinational corporations. In the aggregate, corporate inversions were not meaningful enough to the broader system of US corporate taxation to justify the tax reform that ultimately occurred.

Why weren't corporate inversions more commonplace?

Answer: A few reasons: First, to take advantage of the repatriation benefit, the company needed to have a big pile of accumulated foreign profits and offshore cash. Only some companies were in that situation, largely because many foreign countries have corporate tax rates comparable to that of the United States. For example, if a foreign country levied corporate tax at 35 percent, then the US corporate tax on repatriation would have been 0 percent, because the residual tax is the difference between the foreign tax and the US tax. Second, to take advantage of the interest deduction disallowance, the company had to be highly leveraged in the United States or willing to become highly leveraged. Many US companies did not have uses for surplus cash derived from incremental borrowing, however. For example, let's say that Burger King wanted a tax deduction for paying interest to a bank on a loan the bank gave it. That makes good tax sense, but it does not make practical sense. This is because the company would have to use the cash it received from the loan in some efficient way. For example, if it paid dividends to the shareholders from the borrowed funds, that would result in a shareholder-level tax for some shareholders. Alternately, the company could choose to open more restaurants with the funds, but Burger King surely has already saturated the US market, so that's not practicable either. Basically, companies considering a corporate inversion often did not have executives with novel business ideas on how to reinvest their cash derived from past profits or from borrowing. Therefore, any potential benefit from an increased interest deduction would accrue only to those companies that had found a way to borrow and then spend the cash efficiently, obviously not Burger King. An alternative to inverting the business to Canada might have been to hire corporate executives to lead the company with novel business ideas on how to invest capital in the United States to generate a tax deduction today and profit tomorrow.

Third, when a corporation chose a corporate inversion, this often meant that assets were transferred to the US parent company in exchange for control of the company. So, in the transfer of control from the United States to a new foreign parent—in Burger King's case, the Canadian doughnut chain Tim Hortons—some amount of money was paid into the United States in exchange for that control. The US accounting firm advisors on corporate inversions were extremely creative in devising ways not to transfer anything meaningful into the United States that would generate a tax liability in the future, but this was possible only to some degree, and under certain circumstances, so the inversion transaction was not always practical for firms.

Fourth, the rarity of corporate inversions was because mostly those US multinationals with declining business prospects or poor business models without the need for capital reinvestment were likely to seek out an inversion. In fact, this should be considered the default explanation for a company's inversion, absent some other explanation. In our example, Burger King is a classic example of a US multinational with a declining business model. It appears to have sold control of itself to Tim Hortons because it did not have any other solution to its business problems and declining growth prospects in the United States. The tax aspects of the sale to Tim Hortons were thus essentially a smokescreen. Corporate tax can be avoided by reinvesting profits into a growing business, in the case of Burger King, by, for example, opening more restaurants. However, Americans do not want more Burger King restaurants, so Burger King couldn't avoid taxes that way. The takeaway is that poorly managed businesses or those with declining business models were usually the ones that took advantage of corporate inversion and only a small tax avoidance was achieved.

TRANSFER PRICING

Transfer pricing is the internal sale of production or finished goods to related-party affiliates of the company. The internal transfer of products between divisions of the same company can have drastic tax consequences, and transfer pricing can be used as a means for large multinational corporations to avoid tax liability. As a hypothetical example, transfer pricing on finished goods reflects the "transfer" of finished cars from the General Motors manufacturing affiliate in

Mexico to the sales affiliate in the United States. Because the company controls the price charged for the finished product between the manufacturing and sales affiliate, it can determine the tax consequences to its affiliates in Mexico and the United States by shifting the price charged between its own affiliates. This ability to shift the price—and the resulting profits—is relevant in cases where tax rates are different between the two jurisdictions. For example, if taxes are high in the United States and low in Mexico, then General Motors can charge a high price for cars sold internally (within the company) from Mexico into the United States. The high internal price means that profits in the United States will appear low when the cars are sold to customers. If the tax rate is higher in the United States, then the taxes are reduced because the profit is less because of the low intercompany price, or transfer price. Here is a hypothetical illustration of transfer pricing on finished goods, to maximize profit in Mexico and avoid US taxes:

Mexico Manufacturing Affiliate	US Sales Affiliate	Customer Price
Vehicle Production cost: $2,500	Vehicle Acquisition Cost: $18,000	$20,000
Mexico-to-US Sale Price: $18,000	Customer Sale Price: $20,000	
Mexico Profit: $15,500	US Profit: $2,000	

Here is the same illustration, but *without* transfer pricing:

Mexico Manufacturing Affiliate	US Sales Affiliate	Customer Price
Vehicle Production cost: $2,500	Vehicle Acquisition Cost: $5,000	$20,000
Mexico-to-US Sale Price: $5,000	Customer Sale Price: $20,000	
Mexico Profit: $2,500	US Profit: $15,000	

Multinational firms are accordingly able to use transfer pricing on finished goods as one possible means to avoid taxation. As an illustration, General Motors has not paid any income tax in the United States for many years, and transfer pricing is presumably part of the reason for its lack of tax liability. What is important about this hypothetical is that the overarching concepts are true, even though the details vary by company: this is just the beginning. Transfer pricing can be used not only on finished products, but also on anything that goes into a product.

Such transfer-pricing methods can also be applied on intangibles—such as royalties from product patents and trademarks—to shift the price on products. Intangibles comprise some of the purchase price and value of the ultimate product, often accounting for most of the price and value, depending on the product type. For cars, vehicle manufacturers hold patents on many aspects of vehicle design, such as the engine, transmission, windshield wipers and so on. For example, Mazda produced a rotary engine vehicle for many years because it held the patents on that type of rotary automobile engine and not an in-line automobile engine. If a company produced a vehicle with an in-line piston engine of a certain design, it needed to pay a royalty to the patent holder on that design, which would increase the cost of the cars it produced. Although the rotary engine design was unique, it made sense for Mazda to produce cars with that engine design because it held the patents so did not need to pay any other company royalties.

Vehicle manufacturers also hold trademarks, such as a logo or vehicle name, like "Ford" or the "F-150" truck. These trademarks may not seem significant to customers, but all large multinationals assign significant value to the trademarks and tradenames of their products. Conveniently, for tax purposes, it is possible to use transfer pricing to shift business intangibles into tax havens and then charge local affiliates for the use of those intangibles. This shifting of the ownership of intangibles then reduces taxable income in higher-tax jurisdictions. For large multinational companies, royalties are then often owned in tax haven jurisdictions with a 0 percent tax rate on profits received from royalties. Therefore, as the royalties are designated on the sale of products between affiliates of the same company, the royalty income arises in the tax haven jurisdiction, and the company avoids all tax on the portion of the profit reflected in the royalty. Here is a hypothetical illustration of transfer pricing on intangible royalties used to shift income into the Cayman Islands tax haven in order to maximize profit there:

Mexico Affiliate	**Tax Haven (owns intangibles)**	**US Sales Affiliate**
Vehicle cost: $2,500	Royalty (profit): $7,500	Vehicle cost: $12,500
Royalty cost: $7,500	Tax on royalty: $0	Customer Price: $20,000
Total Cost: ($10,000)		
Mexico Profit: $2,500	Untaxed Profit $7,500	US Profit: $7,500

The use of intangibles is helpful where there is income tax in both countries, such as Mexico and the United States. In this case, Mexico does have some income tax. A special manufacturing zone was created in Mexico's border areas (referred to as the maquiladora regime), which applies a lower tax rate on goods produced within a few miles of the United States, which are then exported to the United States. Although the maquiladora rules were modified in 2014, nearly all US manufacturing companies with production activities in Mexico set up manufacturing plants in the border area to take advantage of the lower Mexican tax rate in this zone. However, it still makes good financial sense to shift income into tax havens using transfer pricing on intangibles in order to avoid even the low income taxes on production in the Mexican maquiladora zones.

Here is a hypothetical illustration of shifting profits using intangibles into a tax haven:

Caymans Affiliate	Netherlands	Coffee Shop (NYC)	Customer Price
Owns Patent	Roasting Facility	Point of Sale	Coffee: $4/cup
Charges 3.79/cup	Pays $3.79/cup	Pays: $3.80/cup	
Tax $0	Charges $3.80/cup	Other costs ($0.19/cup)	
	Profit $0.01/cup	Charges $4.00/cup	
	Tax $0	Profit: $0.01	
		Tax $0	
			Total Tax: $0

Taxable income can be reduced by intercompany transactions, and these are available only to multinational firms that have some level of vertical integration in their business. Starbucks is a good illustration, because the coffee shop business is easy to understand. It is thought that Starbucks historically charged its affiliates for coffee-bean roasting services, so the local affiliate in the United Kingdom, for example, presumably got a local tax deduction that reduced Starbucks' local taxes in the United Kingdom (referred to in tax parlance as the "source" of income or profits). The profit or taxable income from that source was then presumably shifted into a country with a lower tax rate.[10]

The significance of transfer pricing to small businesses operating in competition with large multinational corporations is especially evident in major cities, where Starbucks has replaced local coffee shops who were not able to avoid tax on profits through transfer pricing techniques. Net taxes on the profits of local coffee shops owned by sole proprietors in these jurisdictions often exceed 50 percent or even more. Starbucks' corporate shops pay a far lesser rate—less than 10 percent, or even less than 5 percent. That low effective tax rate is due in part to transfer pricing. Indeed, as various reporters in the United Kingdom discovered through careful investigation, it's hard to say as a matter of tax accounting how much tax Starbucks actually pays on a current basis in any particular country because the tax rate depends on its intercompany charges and whether those transactions are audited, and adjusted, in each country. The low tax rate constitutes a substantial business advantage for Starbucks over small coffee shops that try to compete with Starbucks.

Small businesses are unable to use these income-shifting strategies available to large multinationals. The end result of a tax system that favors large multinational firms is that such firms can consolidate capital and acquire competitors, and thus reduce competition, and then to charge higher prices once the smaller competitors have been eliminated from the marketplace. This partly explains why independent coffee shops have largely been eliminated from the streets of many cities around the world.

As a general rule, if a country does not enforce its transfer-pricing rules, then it will not collect much, if any, tax from multinational firms that have affiliates in other taxing jurisdictions. The above illustrations show how this is possible. The company sets the price on intercompany sales and thereby determines the tax base in each country; of course, different countries have different tax rates, including some that have 0 percent tax, so multinational firms can easily shift income to reduce their tax absent some degree of tax enforcement. The transfer-pricing rules in the United States are contained in § 482 of the Internal Revenue Code. There also exist exceedingly complex regulations and technical guidance on how to set transfer prices. Such rules are necessary in order to police intercompany prices on finished goods, intangibles, manufacturing processes and so on, all of which make it possible to collect tax from large multinational corporations. The transfer-pricing rules have the effect of maintaining the tax base in each country, or the amount of taxable profits from business activity, to which the statutory tax rate will be multiplied to determine tax liability. Absent these rules, very little tax revenue would be collected from multinational firms, irrespective of the corporate tax rate. The statutory corporate tax rate is much less important to the collection of tax revenue from multinational firms than is the enforcement of transfer-pricing rules—the overwhelming tax avoidance method of large firms. The actual enforcement practices of the IRS are discussed in the last section of this chapter.

TAX INCENTIVES FOR SMALL BUSINESS
IN THE TAX CUTS AND JOBS ACT OF 2017

The IRS issued final regulatory guidance on how small business might qualify for the new deduction in January 2019. The Tax Cuts and Jobs Act of 2017 incorporated a new 20 percent deduction for qualifying pass-through businesses. This sounds good, but the devil is in the details. For many small businesses, the 20 percent tax deduction will not reduce their tax liability.[11] For a pass-through entity to claim the new 20 percent deduction, a significant amount of tax planning would be required with a tax accountant or lawyer. Accordingly, even with the final regulations issued, it is generally not possible to know which small businesses qualify without careful study of the details of the business structure of each small business. Tax planning is therefore required because of the extraordinary complexity of the new rules, which require analysis of how the small business owner provides services to the pass-through entity and how he or she is paid for those services. Many small businesses cannot afford to pay an accountant for the degree of tax planning required to formally qualify under these technical provisions. Furthermore, various professional service firms, such as law firms and accounting firms, are automatically excluded from eligibility for the new deduction and will not benefit from it either.

Thus, very few small businesses are likely to gain a significant tax advantage from the additional 20 percent tax deduction for pass-throughs. Although some types of small business are flatly excluded by rule, the broader ineligibility is largely because of a limitation on the availability of the tax deduction based on the amount of W-2 wages paid. For many small business owners, the tax deduction becomes available to the pass-through entity only to the extent of 50 percent of wages paid to the owner. Such a situation is relatively common among small business operations, where the owner works for the pass-through entity. Of course, small businesses might engage in tax planning to increase the proportion of W-2 reportable payments by structuring payments to the small business owner as wages—those wages would be highly taxed as labor income.

The IRS is well aware that labor income is taxed heavily. The purpose of the limitations in the new rule is to encourage—essentially to force—small business owners to pay wages to themselves and thereby incur very high rates of tax on their wage income treated as self-employment income. This allows the pass-through entity to claim the 20 percent deduction, but at the expense of incurring large amounts of wage tax on payments to the small business owner. The regulations are designed to prevent small businesses from claiming the new deduction unless they give up on other tax planning designed to avoid Social

Security tax on some of the small business profits. For small businesses, Social Security tax rates are very high because they include both the employer and employee portions; this is referred to as the self-employment tax.[12] As a general rule of thumb, many small businesses could restructure payments to the owners as wages, but then they would pay self-employment tax on that amount. This would ultimately cancel out much of the benefit from the deduction, so the new law is not helpful for small business that already had performed some limited amount of tax planning mainly to avoid the self-employment tax.

To summarize, the IRS wrote the eligibility rules for the new 20 percent deduction for pass-throughs in a very restrictive way to penalize any small businesses not paying self-employment tax at shockingly high tax rates. The elimination of this type of tax avoidance planning by small businesses to minimize the amount of wages paid to owners performing services for the pass-through seems to have always been the primary objective of the IRS. The new regulations continue what amounts to the IRS's proxy war against small business owners on behalf of large corporations. The objective of the proxy war is to eliminate as many small businesses as possible, especially in markets where they compete with large corporations. Once the little guys are out of the picture, then large corporations are able to set higher prices—and with the higher prices the US government then steps in to report economic "growth" has occurred as the price level has increased. The reality is that consumers have become less well-off to the extent that larger corporations have increased the price level for products but average wages have not increased to that extent. In many local communities, consumers are better off with small businesses operating in the marketplace given the price competition with Walmart, as example.

THE LACK OF SMALL BUSINESS TAX NEUTRALITY

The new 20 percent tax deduction for pass-throughs allowed politicians to claim that a tax benefit was made available to small business via the tax reform. The tax reform had only a nominal substantive benefit to small businesses, however. The tax reform bill obviously allowed significant benefits to big business by reducing the corporate statutory tax rate from 35 percent to 21 percent. The extraordinary problem of the new design of the tax system is that it does not include any concept of small business tax neutrality. That is, a significant aspect of how tax policy is designed is to compare horizontally how various types of businesses are taxed under a particular tax proposal. This is a matter not so much of horizontal equity, or fairness, but of horizontal competitiveness, where taxes represent a significant part of the competitive business environment, especially for small businesses. The lack of tax neutrality for small businesses creates an extraordinary problem in the tax system: If the corporate rate is less than the pass-through rate, as it surely is (the corporate rate is 21 percent, and the individual rate about 39 percent or so depending on income level), then the corporate shell has a lower statutory rate than the small business does for current profits. This allows for the corporation to automatically defer taxation inside the shell. The deferral within the corporate shell is not efficient for the economy if the corporation does not reinvest the profit into new business pursuits. Large corporations are less likely to invest profits into new business pursuits than small businesses, so it is reasonable to conclude that setting the corporate rate too low relative to the small business tax rate would tend to *inhibit* economic growth.

The predominant determinant of efficiency in the tax system is not the degree to which taxes reduce the return on capital investment, as most economists believe, but rather how or whether the rate structure encourages or discourages the reinvestment of profits by profitable businesses. That reinvestment of profit is what *causes* incremental economic growth. This is notably a *scientific* view and claim about tax policy because it can be tested with evidence. The effects of tax reform then need to be evaluated along these lines. The Tax Cuts and Jobs Act of 2017 has the effect of reducing the incentive for large corporations to make capital reinvestments in order to gain a tax deduction. For the reasons already stated, small businesses likely did not gain much or anything from the tax reform, notwithstanding the creation of the new 20 percent deduction for pass-throughs. Therefore, large corporations gained an even more substantial tax benefit vis-à-vis their small business competitors. In fact, the tax cuts for large corporations are likely to *cause* a recession (once any stimulative effect from increased cash in the economy wears off) and not create economic growth. The tax cuts are a disincentive for profitable firms to reinvest profits into new business lines because of the diminished value of tax deductions for capital reinvestment by large, already profitable firms.

ENFORCEMENT OF CORPORATE TAX LAWS

Corporate tax laws are generally not enforced for the IRS to raise revenue. The IRS does not set out to raise revenue by identifying the tax issues of large corporations and seeking to assess tax, as it does with individual taxpayers. In tax law, what matters most is not which laws are on the books but which tax laws are enforced by the authorities. Tax laws are enforced through audit or threat of audit.[13] Usually enforcement is important for laws, but for taxation there is a self-reporting system of compliance. Taxpayers file taxes on an honor system. Transfer pricing by multinational firms likewise proceeds on an honor system, one that is often not subject to audit. The IRS tends to automatically accept the submitted numbers. Therefore, determining which taxpayers to audit, and how, is of extraordinary significance for the tax system to collect revenue.

As it turns out, the IRS has adopted what it calls a "policy of restraint" in tax audits solely for large corporations. The policy of restraint means that the auditor does not check internal accounting records—what are known as FIN48 records—as part of the audit.[14] These are mandatory accounting records maintained by public companies on tax issues. However, the IRS does not typically request the FIN48 records as part of the audit process of large corporations pursuant to its so-called policy of restraint for large public companies.[15] For example, if a large corporation is engaged in tax structuring in furtherance of an inversion transaction, the internal company records relevant to tax issues needed for the preparation of the financial statements would not be reviewed by the IRS during the course of the company tax audit.

The corporate tax system is thus not enforced by the IRS so as to raise revenue; if it were, then the IRS would audit large corporations on the basis of their FIN48 records. It does not, and the reason it does not appears to be related to the deception of the delicate hummingbird (see the introduction). That is, the IRS seems to hold the idea that if large corporations had to pay some tax, they would just pack up and leave. This is false; corporations will not leave if there is a profit to be made, even if the profit is partly reduced by taxes—any marginal profit is still profit. Yet for individual taxpayers, the concern over taxpayers leaving the United States with aggressive tax enforcement is not raised; Congress even ordered the IRS to restrain itself in the heavy-handed audit tactics directed against small businesses and individual taxpayers,[16] and it even created the Taxpayer Advocate Service to this end. However, the Taxpayer Advocate Service, which was chartered by Congress as an agency within the IRS as tasked to protect individual taxpayers, has used much of its funding to foster an initiative referred to as "cooperative compliance," which is designed exclusively for the benefit of large corporations. Under the cooperative compliance program in force in the United States referred to as the "CAP program", the corporate audit is restricted in various respects, including especially the lack of review of internal accounting documents for tax structuring.[17] These restrictions on corporate audits seem to have been extremely lucrative for large corporations in avoiding tax adjustments on audit.[18] A similar cooperative compliance initiative solely for large corporations also gained significant traction in several European nations, including the Netherlands and the United Kingdom.[19]

THE LACK OF ENFORCEMENT OF
ACCUMULATED EARNINGS TAX

Other parts of the tax reform also reflect the lack of tax enforcement against large corporations. This is especially true for taxes on the repatriation of overseas corporate earnings.[20] The repatriation of these funds would have caused the accrual of US tax liability under prior law, roughly equal to the net of the historical US tax rate (35 percent) less the foreign tax (e.g., 20 percent) already paid on those earnings (15 percent). However, the Tax Cuts and Jobs Act of 2017 allowed a reduced, flat rate for repatriation, from roughly 8 percent to 5 percent.[21] Thus, instead of paying the tax on repatriation, multinational firms have repatriated $465 billion under the reduced rate, thus far. This will likely increase to $2.5 trillion once the IRS finalizes and clarifies all the applicable rules.[22] This means that the tax reform not only provided cuts to the corporate rate (from 35 percent to 21 percent) but *also* helped large corporations avoid paying very much tax on repatriation—and they had wanted to avoid paying tax on the repatriation of foreign profits that had been accumulating for roughly fifteen years.

Yet, the US tax laws already provide an accumulated earnings tax.[23] This tax on accumulations applies when a corporation does not reinvest corporate profits or pay dividends to shareholders. It should have been applied on the $2 trillion or so of large firms' accumulated offshore earnings, at a minimum rate of 20 percent. However, the IRS enforces the accumulated earnings tax only against small- and medium-sized businesses, not against large multinational corporations, even though the accumulated tax is on the books as applying for all corporations, large and small.[24]

The amount of uncollected tax from the lack of enforcement of the accumulated earnings tax is staggering. It is sad that whenever the accumulated earnings tax is enforced against a small- to midsize company, which is not uncommon, the US tax system becomes extremely unfair in its favoritism of large corporations over small businesses. Often, family-owned corporations fail to pay dividends because they can easily transfer stock to other family members as part of estate planning. The IRS then targets the accumulation of profits within a family corporation, and this is a common application of the accumulated earnings tax. But large corporations have trillions of dollars in cash stashed offshore—*trillions*—much more than a family corporation.[25] The equal protection clause of the US Constitution should apply in order to prevent this type of double standard; if the law does not apply against large corporations, then it should not apply against smaller firms.

The IRS often does not enforce the existing tax laws against large corporations. The unenforced laws that are already on the books would require those corporations to pay dividends back to the United States from overseas affiliates or be subject to residual tax. If the corporations chose to pay dividends, this would attract some residual tax, totaling probably between $400 billion and $600 billion—much more than has been collected pursuant to the Tax Cuts and Jobs Act of 2017. The avoidance of tax on overseas profits constitutes a significant amount of money that could be contributing to pay off the national debt of the United States. That money is legitimately owed to the United States by the large corporations that have accrued overseas profits, often in tax havens, yet the IRS chooses not to collect it. Leading tax scholars and tax attorneys in the United States are fully aware that those overseas profits should have been subjected to tax under the accumulated earnings tax, yet nobody says a word.

THE DECEPTION OF "CORPORATE TAX COMPETITION"

All over the world, governments have increasingly embraced a wrongheaded tax policy idea: corporate tax competition.[26] This term refers to reducing tax rates on big business in an attempt to increase national economic growth. Whichever country sets the lowest corporate tax rates wins. Economists sometimes refer to the type of economic competition this may create as a slippery slope where countries try to outdo themselves to lower taxes on large corporations.

Does the idea of corporate tax competition make any sense? To find out, we might ask whether multinational firms tend to make capital investments into lower-taxed countries. The answer is no, which may at first be surprising. Ask yourself whether you've ever heard of a manufacturing company opening an automated factory to manufacture automobiles—or really any product—in the Bahamas, Panama, or Malta, all of which have very low corporate tax rates. Absolutely not. Malta, for example, has tried to establish itself as a hub for the new industry of online gaming because it is not competitive at all for established industries in higher-taxed companies. How could this be?

The truth is that capital investment by multinational firms generally flows into higher-taxed countries, such as Finland, Japan, Korea, Germany, the United States, India, China, France and so on. But if tax rates are favorable in tax havens, why doesn't capital investment migrate into tax havens so that the centers of world commerce would be, say, Nassau, Panama City and Valetta, instead of New York, Tokyo and London? When it comes time to deploy capital, the capital nearly always makes its way back into the higher-tax countries to build factories. Infrastructure might play some role in this, but the most important reason is that the tax system is set up differently for large multinational corporations than for individual workers and small businesses.

Consider the following: A multinational firm needs to decide whether to locate an automated factory that produces televisions in Korea, where the taxes are extremely high, or in Panama, where the taxes are extremely low. Both countries are similar with respect to infrastructure, utility costs and so on. Where will the firm locate the factory? Korea. The reason for this is that the multinational firm gets a tax deduction for capital outlay on the factory and can deduct that cost up-front or over time as depreciation. The tax deductions reduce taxable income, and that reduction is worth more to the multinational corporation, not less, in the higher-tax jurisdiction, where the multinational firm is already a taxpayer. Tax deductions are actually worth nothing if the tax rate is 0 percent. Multinational firms are also not as concerned as many economists think about taxes on future profits because they can use transfer pricing to eliminate profits in Korea when it comes time to sell some new televisions all over the world. So, bottom line, a multinational corporation that is profitable in Korea would make a capital investment into Korea rather than a tax haven such as Panama to reduce the taxes it already pays by netting depreciable costs against income.

NOTES

1 Internal Revenue Service, *Proposed Regulations on 20% Deduction for Small Business*, https://www.irs.gov/newsroom/irs-issues-proposed-regulations-on-new-20-percent-deduction-for-passthrough-businesses. Accessed Nov. 10, 2019.

2 *GOP Leaders Reach Tax Deal, Cutting Corporate Rate to 21% and Top Individual Rate to 37%*, LA Times (Dec. 13, 2017), www.latimes.com/politics/la-na-pol-gop-tax-plan-20171213-story.html. Accessed Nov. 10, 2019.

3 For a detailed explanation of the congressional scoring process, see Adam Fletcher & Trenton Hamilton, *Scoring and Revenue Estimation*, http://www.law.harvard.edu/faculty/hjackson/ScoringRevenueEstimation_5(rev).pdf. Accessed Nov. 10, 2019.

4 For a discussion of the supposed macroeconomic feedback of corporate tax cuts, see Benjamin R. Page et al., *Macroeconomic Analysis of the Tax Cuts and Jobs Act*, www.taxpolicycenter.org/sites/default/files/publication/151176/2001651-macroeconomic_analysis_of_the_tax_cuts_and_jobs_act.pdf. Accessed Nov. 10, 2019.

5 See Bret N. Bogenschneider, *A Theory of Small Business Tax Neutrality*, 15 FSU Bus. Rev. 33 (2016).

6 See Bret Wells, *What Corporate Inversions Teach About International Tax Reform*, 127:12 Tax Notes 1345 (2010); but see Bret N. Bogenschneider, *Why Corporate Inversions Are Irrelevant to U.S. Tax Policy*, 146 Tax Notes 1267 (2015).

7 See Vauhini Vara, *Is the Burger King–Tim Hortons Deal About More Than Taxes*, New Yorker (Aug. 26, 2014); Devin Leonard, *Burger King Is Run by Children*, Bloomberg News (July 24, 2014).

8 For an example of misleading news reports suggesting that corporate inversions reflect bad tax policy, see *Corporate Inversions Are the Symptoms, Bad Tax Policy Is the Disease*, Forbes (March 8, 2016), https://www.forbes.com/sites/econostats/2016/03/08/corporate-inversions-are-the-symptoms-bad-tax-policy-is-the-disease/#6dc33add5366. Accessed Nov. 10, 2019.

9 Internal Revenue Code § 312.

10 See Tom Bergin, *Special Report: How Starbucks Avoids UK Taxes*, Reuters (Oct. 15, 2012), uk.reuters.com/article/us-britain-starbucks-tax/special-report-how-starbucks-avoids-uk-taxes-idUKBRE89E0EX20121015 ("Presented with the contradiction between Starbucks' UK accounts and its comments to investors, Starbucks' CFO Alstead identified two factors at play, both related to payments between companies within the group. The first is royalties on intellectual property […] Alstead said some of the unit's revenue was also paid to other Starbucks units, including one in Switzerland.").

11 See Jim Puzzanghera & James Rufus Koren, *The Republican Tax Bill's Small-Business Problem: Most Won't Benefit from the Special New Rate*, LA Times (Nov. 3, 2017), www.latimes.com/business/la-fi-pass-through-taxes-20171103-story.html. Accessed Nov. 10, 2019.

12 Internal Revenue Code § 1401, et seq.

13 The IRS enforcement budget has been significantly reduced in recent years, and Congress has simultaneously mandated audits of working poor persons who claim the earned income tax credit. See Paul Kiel & Jesse Eisenger, *How the IRS Was Gutted* (Dec. 11, 2018), https://www.propublica.org/article/how-the-irs-was-gutted. Accessed Nov. 10, 2019 ("Corporations and the wealthy are the biggest beneficiaries of the IRS' decay. Most Americans' interaction with the IRS is largely automated. But it takes specialized, well-trained personnel to audit a business or a billionaire or to unravel a tax scheme […] For the country's largest corporations, the danger of being hit with a billion-dollar tax bill has greatly diminished […] Under continued pressure from Republicans, the IRS has long made a priority of auditing people who receive that money, and as the IRS has shrunk, those audits have consumed even more resources, accounting for 36 percent of audits last year. The credit's recipients—whose annual income is typically less than $20,000—are now examined at rates similar to those who make $500,000 to $ 1 million a year. Only people with incomes above $ 1 million are examined much more frequently.").

14 IRS Uncertain Tax Positions: Modified Policy of Restraint (Mar. 23, 2011), Memorandum for Large Business & International Employees, Large Business & International Division ("Accordingly, LB&I examiners cannot request, in any open examination, documents that are privileged under the attorney-client privilege, the tax advice privilege, or the work product doctrine, notwithstanding whether these documents have been provided to an independent auditor as part of a financial statement audit unless the privilege has been otherwise waived. Any outstanding requests for such documents should be withdrawn."), https://www.irs.gov/businesses/corporations/uncertain-tax-positions-modified-policy-of-restraint. Accessed Nov. 10, 2019. See also Financial Accounting Standards Board (FASB), *FIN48 Summary*, www.fasb.org/summary/finsum48.shtml. Accessed Nov. 10, 2019 ("The evaluation of a tax position in accordance with this Interpretation is a two-step process. The first step

is recognition: The enterprise determines whether it is more likely than not that a tax position will be sustained upon examination. [...] The second step is measurement: A tax position that meets the more-likely-than-not recognition threshold is measured to determine the amount of benefit to recognize in the financial statements.").

15 IRS Memorandum for Executives, Managers, and Examiners, Large and Mid-Size Business Division, LMSB-04-0507-044 May 10, 2007, FIN48 and Tax Accrual Workpapers ("We have received a determination from Counsel that FIN 48 Workpapers are Tax Accrual Workpapers, and they are therefore subject to our current policy of restraint.").

16 See Taxpayer Bill of Rights, included in the Technical and Miscellaneous Revenue Act of 1988 (TAMRA), Pub. L. No. 100647.

17 Bret N. Bogenschneider, *A Revised Theory of the Corporate Tax Audit: Toward non-Cooperative Compliance*, Capital Univ. L. Rev. (forthcoming 2020); but see Leigh Osofsky, *The Case Against Strategic Tax Law Uncertainty*, 64 Tax L. Rev. 489 (2011).

18 See Max de Haldevang, Quartz. Yahoo! Finance. *Walmart Dodged Up to $2.6 Billion in US Tax Through a "Fictitious" Chinese Entity, Former Executive Says*, https://finance.yahoo.com/news/walmart-dodged-2-6-billion-151531554.html. Accessed Nov. 10, 2019.

19 Erich Kirchler, Cristoph Kogler & Stephan Muehlbacher, *Cooperative Tax Compliance*, 23:2 Curr. Dir. Psych. Science 87–92 (Apr. 2014) ("Whereas enforced compliance depends on the power of authorities, voluntary cooperation originates from taxpayers' trust in the authorities. [...] The psychological approach to tax behavior has led to a change in tax authorities' practices for regulating citizen behavior. Under the labels of 'enhanced relationships,' 'horizontal monitoring,' and 'fair-play initiatives,' several European countries are advancing cooperative strategies with taxpayers.").

20 See as amended Tax Cuts and Jobs Act of 2017, Internal Revenue Code § 965. Treatment of Deferred Foreign Income upon Transition to Participation Exemption System of Taxation.

21 The reduced rate is either 5 percent or 8 percent, depending on whether accumulated foreign earnings were reinvested or held in cash. The standard residual US repatriation tax would have been up to 35 percent. Broadly speaking, the amount of repatriation tax was the US corporate rate (35 percent, historically) less any foreign taxes paid on the earnings (E&P). This amount is typically close to 0 percent, as multinational firms carefully plan to have available pools of low-taxed E&P in order to take advantage in the case of the holiday (as with the Tax Cuts and Jobs Act of 2017).

22 Repatriated profits total $465 billion after Trump tax cuts, leaving $2.5 trillion overseas. Jeffry Bartash, *Repatriated Profits Total $465 Billion After Trump Tax Cuts—Leaving $2.5 Trillion Overseas* (Sept. 19, 2018), www.marketwatch.com/story/repatriated-profits-total-nearly-500-billion-after-trump-tax-cuts-2018-09-19. Accessed Nov. 10, 2019.

23 IRC § 531, et. seq. Accumulated Earnings Tax.

24 *See* Bret N. Bogenschneider, *A Proposal for Equal Enforcement of the AET*, 147 Tax Notes 931 (May 25, 2015).

25 Katia Dmitrieva & Laura Davison, *Corporate America Is Repatriating a Fraction of Foreign Profits*, Bloomberg (June 20, 2019), https://www.bloomberg.com/amp/news/articles/2019-06-20/corporate-america-is-repatriating-a-fraction-of-foreign-profits.

Accessed Nov. 10, 2019 ("The cash that has come back to the U.S. falls short of the $4 trillion President Donald Trump said would return as a result of the 2017 tax law. Investment banks and think tanks have estimated that U.S. corporations actually held $ 1.5 trillion to $2.5 trillion in offshore funds at the time the law was enacted.").

26 See Michael Devereux & Simon Loretz, *What Do We Know About Corporate Tax Competition?*, Oxford Whitepaper, http://eureka.sbs.ox.ac.uk/4386/1/WP1229.pdf. Accessed Nov. 10, 2019.

CHAPTER 4

THE LIMITS OF MORAL PHILOSOPHY IN FORMULATING TAX POLICY

Chapter Summary: *Moral philosophy as applied to taxation is inadequate because it fails to specify a means to count the results. For example, moral standards offer no method of accounting to determine the amount of tax that a given person has paid. In the applied field of taxation, a method of counting is a prerequisite to reach any moral conclusions about right and wrong. This inability to count the beans renders moral philosophy practically useless in the formation of tax policy, as it is only by counting consequences that the bulk of any moral framework can be revealed. In the end, current moral standards applied to tax policy might apply only at the far edges of debate where no counting is needed to determine answers. Since the fairness of tax results nearly always depends on counted results, claims of right and wrong in taxation are only rendered feasible by incorporating an external means by which to count beans. In addition, some moral questions, such as the deferral of taxation of capital income but not labor income, become visible only through accounting by the process of counting the beans, and so have been largely missed by moral philosophers writing on the topic of tax fairness absent accounting methods. The use of a cash-basis method of accounting makes it obvious that workers currently pay most taxes in modern society, which largely obfuscates the conclusions by famous philosophers on matters of tax policy, including John Rawls. Other tax philosophers, such as Richard Epstein, simply switch back and forth between various standards of moral philosophy to reach bizarre (supposedly libertarian) conclusions that taxes paid by the wealthy are bad, but taxes paid by workers are fine and dandy. To the contrary, as a matter of Libertarian theory, taxes on productive work should generally be disfavored as workers are entitled to hold at least some portion of the wealth derived from their work even if that means at times switching the rank-order of persons in wealth holdings not derived from productive work; absent an accounting method it's impossible to rank-order persons in wealth holdings anyway.*

The type of philosophy most often applied to taxation and the formation of tax policy is moral philosophy.[1] Examples of moral philosophy are libertarianism, utilitarianism, liberalism, economics and religion. The goal of moral philosophy is to establish what is "just" or "right" with regard to tax policy. The process of engaging in moral philosophy is altering what counts as a consequence in identifying justice or rightness in respect of taxation.[2] For example, utilitarian theory looks at the maximization of utility as measured by pleasure and pain. In economic theory, efficiency is often what counts, whereas Rawlsian philosophy counts the welfare of persons in society.[3] The choice between types of moral philosophy is critically important to the field of taxation because making decisions based on evidence is extremely rare when it comes to formulating tax policy. For example—as we've been discovering throughout this book—the available evidence indicates that higher taxes are strongly associated with higher rates of economic growth, yet tax policymakers work to further corporate tax competition and tax cuts, believing that lower corporate tax rates are just or right. Whether or not this belief is empirically true, it is premised foremost on moral philosophy, not evidence or science. Thus, the choice of moral philosophy in formulating tax policy is exceedingly important. Furthermore, since the standards for what counts as a consequence varies between the types of philosophy, the initial choice of moral philosophy often determines the end result. As it stands today, the moral frameworks of libertarianism, liberalism and economic theory are the moral philosophies that tax policymakers turn to most often for determining what counts as a consequence in tax policy.

THE ROLE OF ACCOUNTING METHODS IN MORAL PHILOSOPHY AND TAXATION

All standards of moral philosophy used in taxation can be adjusted (or mediated) to specific situations in taxation only by the application of some *external* method of accounting.[4] However, such method is rarely or never disclosed in philosophical analyses of taxation. Many of the heated philosophical debates around taxation and tax policy can be understood merely as disagreements about how benefits or burdens should be counted within a particular method of accounting.[5] These debates have obviously revealed disagreements among philosophy previously applied to tax policy, including that of John Locke, Richard Posner, Robert Nozick and so on.[6] In many situations, moral philosophy has not actually broached the topic of tax fairness in any realistic way, however, because fairness becomes visible only when a method of accounting has been determined and consistently applied in the respective analysis. Simply put, some issues of moral philosophy can become known only by carefully counting beans.

Furthermore, the results can only be determined when a method of tax accounting is *consistently applied* to a particular topic. Many prior philosophical debates on tax policy have featured inconsistent applications of accounting methods. For example, an inconsistent method of counting beans would be to say that future benefits accrued in return for current tax payments should be counted with respect to only workers, and not with respect to large corporations or the wealthy. This is to say that the substantive content of moral philosophy is revealed by the method of accounting and these methods are often external to the moral standard itself; such methods must also be consistently applied by philosophers in order to coherently discuss right and wrong in tax policy.

To understand the difficulties of moral philosophy and how it can be useful only at the edges of the debate, consider this hypothetical:

> A moral internet industrialist has cornered the market on internet search and accumulated a vast fortune. The fortune comprises a significant portion of all the wealth accumulation for the entire society in the aggregate. The industrialist can choose whether to pay taxes or not—either because the tax laws are indeterminate or the industrialist can find a way to avoid paying them. Any taxes paid would be used for the common defense, scientific research, education, and transfer payments (e.g., welfare), but it is impossible to determine which proportion paid would go to each. Assume that the vast majority of society works very hard for little relative pay and pays a high tax rate. Many children (roughly 45%) live at or below the poverty line.

So, should the moral internet industrialist choose to pay tax? The hypothetical actually cannot be answered as it stands under the moral frameworks of liberalism, libertarianism, economic theory, or even Marxist economic theory because each of these frameworks for knowing right and wrong lacks an explicit method of accounting. Moral analysis can begin only with adding additional criteria for counting or some sort of accounting method. For example, under a liberal approach, the welfare gains from any taxes the industrialist pays would be used to improve the standing of the least well-off. But in this hypothetical, we lack the means to make that determination because we lack the ability to count beans. Under a libertarian approach, we would like to assess the incentive effects of work to the commonwealth in the case the industrialist pays taxes, but we also lack the means to do that because we cannot count beans. Under an economic approach, we would assess possible efficiency gains to society, especially from nonpayment of the tax, but again, we lack the means to do any efficiency analysis because we cannot count beans. In Marxist economics, we would need to assess whether the tax might allow others to productively work and achieve self-realization through productivity. We surely lack the means to do that.

Moral analysis is generally impossible without substantive content revealed by bean counting. Absent an accounting method of some sort only general conclusions can be made at the edges. Therefore, we need to begin to add details into the framework of moral analysis, always and predominantly using accounting methods, but also by referring to other relevant local factors, which might include tax laws, demography, statistics, geopolitical relations and so on. No matter what, though, a method of accounting for tax will always be necessary and it must therefore be explicitly stated as part of the methodology of any supposed moral framework applied to tax policy.

ILLUSTRATION OF THE INVENTION OF A NEW METHOD OF ACCOUNTING TO REACH A BIZARRE RESULT: THE CBO'S CALCULATION OF EFFECTIVE TAX RATES

You might think that the Congressional Budget Office (CBO) would serve as a fair and independent body to determine tax consequences given its name and the smart and highly qualified staff who perform its calculations. You'd be wrong. Both political parties in the United States who oversee the CBO broadly agree that taxes should be paid by workers and not by the wealthy or large corporations if and to the extent possible. In Washington even the term "bipartisan," when used in respect to tax policy, implies an alliance against working people to have them pay exceedingly high rates of tax; simultaneously, usage of the term "bipartisan" signals a collective agreement between both political parties to fund the federal budget by effectively robbing the cash contents of the Social Security Trust Fund (which is in effect the collective savings from prior generations of American workers). Because the Social Security Trust Fund is now depleted and cannot be used to balance the cash flows for federal spending, politicians will surely raise taxes on working people either immediately or in the future in order to continue to fund the federal government at current levels.

In 2012, the CBO deceived the public by creating statistics to make it seem as if the wealthy were paying taxes at rates similar to the working poor. The reason they had to create such a deception in the first place is rather obvious— Congress would not want the American people to know that the wealthy actually pay a very low effective tax rate. So, the CBO switched the accounting method for taxes paid in order to hype, or manipulate, the numerator in the equation. The CBO performed this trick as follows:

$$\text{CBO Effective Tax Rate} = \frac{Numerator}{Denominator} = \frac{Taxes\ Paid\ by\ the\ Wealthy}{Taxable\ Income\ of\ the\ Wealthy} + \frac{+\ (plus)\ corporate\ level\ taxes\ paid}{No\ Increase\ (!!!)}$$

Step 1. Add in corporate taxes to the numerator positing these amounts as "taxes" paid by the wealthy.

In order to make it seem as if the wealthy pay a significant amount of taxes, the CBO determined that it should add into the numerator the total amount of taxes paid by large corporations during the year and count these as if they had been paid by the shareholders.[7] Because the wealthy own the vast majority of the corporate stock, this accounting method has the effect of increasing solely the taxes paid by the wealthy in the effective tax rate calculation. Obviously, this reflects a change in accounting methods that is a means of potential deception in the formulation of tax policy.

Notably, this approach taken by the CBO is not itself a reasonable accounting methodology, as it appears to be premised on the idea of offsetting the supposed "double taxes" paid (by large corporations and then by shareholders) and thereby making changes to the method of accounting specifically designed for one category of taxpayer. Other similar adjustments could be made for other categories of taxpayers who pay taxes indirectly, such as consumers. Nearly all economists believe that consumers pay corporate income taxes indirectly through higher prices charged for consumer products produced and sold by corporations. Furthermore, in the prior chapter, it was explained that calling corporation taxation "double taxation" really does not make much sense. Workers are the ones most often subjected to double taxation because they pay income taxes on the portion of their wage income withheld as wage taxes, which they never even receive! The CBO's method is plainly unreasonable, but the real accounting magic happens in the second step.

Step 2. Fail to add in Taxable Income of Corporations for that period to the denominator.

The next step is as follows: The CBO did not include in the denominator of the equation the corresponding taxable income of the corporation for that year. This mismatch resulting from making mismatched changes between the numerator and the denominator is what tax practitioners call a "hype."

There is no legal or mathematical basis for this hype in Step 2 whatsoever—it is completely unjustifiable nonsense. The statistics are misleading because corporations do not pay all profits to shareholders as dividends each year, but instead "retain earnings," which mean they retain most of their profits. This means the portion of corporate profits that are not paid out to shareholders, which is usually the entirety or vast majority of profits (as corporations rarely pay out all profits to shareholders). What this means for the calculation of the effective tax rate is that corporate taxes are included in the numerator, but the denominator includes only the very small portion of shareholder income resulting from dividends paid—it does not include the full amount of corporate profits for the year! Accordingly, the effective tax rate calculated for the wealthy constitutes a wild and ridiculous overstatement. There is no possible explanation for such a misstatement except that it was done intentionally to mislead the American people.

ILLUSTRATION OF A HIDDEN ISSUE OF TAX FAIRNESS REVEALED BY ACCOUNTING METHODS

Automatic deferral of taxation on capital appreciation

A significant characteristic of the modern-day tax system is that capital appreciation is generally taxed only upon what's known as a "tax recognition event." That event refers to a time when tax might be collected at some point in the future or not at all. For example, as a stock appreciates in value, the appreciation is not taxed until the point when the stock is sold. The concept is significant because its application results in very little tax being collected from the wealthy as owners of appreciated capital assets—so little is collected in fact that the IRS seems to hide the data on collected capital gains taxes especially during economic downturns. The owners of capital do not need to do anything to benefit from this type of deferral, so the tax method is essentially "automatic." There are also some opportunities for the owners of capital assets to defer taxation even upon a tax recognition event by tax planning, which is not automatic, such as a "like kind exchange" where one piece of appreciated real estate is traded for another.[8] Furthermore, if a person dies owning property there is a "step up" in basis, where the basis is increased to the asset's fair market value at the date of the owner's death, so that heirs do not need to pay tax on the appreciation in the value of the capital asset. So, basically appreciation in capital assets may never be taxed even upon death, and all this occurs automatically in the tax system as currently designed.

The concept of "automatic deferral" on appreciation in capital assets is illustrated here, using the example of a commercial office building purchased on January 1, 2019:

Purchase Price:	Value Year 2	Capital Gain	Tax
$150 million	$155 million	$5 million	$0
	Value Year 3		
	$165 million	$10 million	$0
	Value Year 4		
	$200 million	$35 million	$0

As long as the capital asset—in this case, the building—is not sold, the appreciation (or capital gain) is not taxed. In addition, the property may function as a tax shelter. This is because the hypothetical depreciation that is posited for tax purposes can offset rental income from the property. The tax shelter is illustrated as follows:

Purchase Price:	Value Year 2	Capital Gain	Rents	Depreciation	Tax
$150 million	$155 million	$5 million	$3 million	($4 million)	$0
	Value Year 3				
	$165 million	$10 million	$3 million	($4 million)	$0
	Value Year 4				
	$200 million	$35 million	$3 million	($4 million)	$0
Total		$50 million	$9 million		$0

This illustration shows that the building accrues a gain that is not taxed, and all of the rental income is also not taxed. So, if the depreciation exceeds the rental income, the difference creates a "shelter," including for other income besides rent. Moral philosophers interested in taxation and tax policy might ask whether that sounds fair at all under the various standards of fairness which they have previously invented often without any method for counting beans.

Although tax deferral is perhaps the most important practical topic in taxation and tax policy, it seems to have been mentioned in the context of moral philosophy only once, and then immediately dismissed. Richard Epstein wrote,

"Deferment looks wealth-enhancing and, hence, Pareto-superior [...] but the debate here would not be on the soundness of the general criteria, but on their application to a particular case—a second order problem."[9] Not exactly.

As mentioned earlier, without a means to count beans, fairness in the tax context can be determined only at the far edges of the debate, where counting is unnecessary. Therefore, in the best-case scenario for moral philosophy, once policymakers decide on a tax policy proposal, trained accountants and tax lawyers can step in to determine whether results are "just" in specific contexts by counting beans in the manner specified by the policymakers' selected moral framework. The applicable accounting methodology is a prerequisite to the consistent application of the moral standard. In other words, there is no separating the counting method from the moral standard, and thereby, to place moral standards as the "first order" and counting beans as the "second order" as Epstein proposes. It actually is not possible to say that preserving the rank-order of persons in wealth holdings is the first order because that rank-order cannot be known without a means to count beans. For example, under a cash-basis method of accounting for beans, a person with a social security pension but a smaller bank account can be ranked lower. But, the accrual value of the future pension payments today is needed to determine the rank under a noncash-basis method of counting beans. Therefore, we actually cannot perform a rank-ordering of persons without first agreeing on a method to count beans.

If a method of accounting for consequences is missing from moral philosophy, then prior attempts to determine tax "fairness" can't even be considered true applications of "philosophy." Prior conclusions purporting to be philosophical, such as the idea that "deferment [of taxation of capital] looks wealth-enhancing and, hence, Pareto-superior" seem to conflate the moral standards of economics with libertarian standards of justice. Pareto superiority means of course that someone might be made better off without making anyone worse off. In switching methods between economics and libertarianism a trick has been performed intending to deceive the reader into thinking that a moral conclusion has been reached as a matter of libertarianism when really all that has happened is that the applicable method has been switched from libertarianism over to economics, and then relabeled the results as "libertarian." Obviously, economics deals with efficiency standards, such as Pareto optimality,[10] and substituting the methodology of economics for libertarianism tells us nothing about the morality of a tax system under the libertarian moral standards. Furthermore, such an approach of switching between methods is not strictly philosophy as the analysis depends mainly on a trick in switching the method without disclosure. Once the switch is disclosed the reader would immediately see that nothing has been said about libertarian theory, for example. It follows that any disguised switch in the method of accounting applied in discussing taxation or tax policy has the intellectual significance of a card trick.

In the popular media, discussions of taxation and tax policy are often in the nature of "card tricks." For example, a double-switch card trick has been invented to make ridiculous claims, such as "Only the rich pay taxes." The double-switch card trick is performed by offsetting taxes paid in the current period against a future accrual of some sort. The offset nets the tax remittance amounts to nothing (or even a negative amount). In order for the trick to work it must be inconsistently applied so that only workers are subjected to "offsets" and never large corporations or the wealthy. The second switch is then to perversely switch again the accounting method applied in the future period to not count worker cash tax remittances in that period either. The method effectively assumes that all future taxes will be paid by the wealthy as opposed to workers—categorically absurd, of course. Hence, where a philosopher or politician proposes that a tax policy is "just" or "fair" by applying a cash-basis method of accounting for one group of taxpayers, and an accrual-basis method of accounting for another group of taxpayers, the supposedly "philosophical" conclusions are a type of rhetoric or political gamesmanship generally comprising a means to fool the innocent and take their money. And, almost nothing about these perverse and rhetorical "card tricks" so often used in debating tax policy comprises "philosophy" or anything approaching a consistent method of accounting.

RESTATEMENT OF ENLIGHTENMENT-ERA THOUGHT ON TAXATION VIA ACCOUNTING METHODS

The moral philosophy of taxation, which often reflects libertarian ideals, generally begins with the positing of a simplified society created by mankind out of the "state of nature" for the common defense and welfare—a commonwealth. The use of taxation to ensure the survival of the commonwealth has also been given as a justification for taxation. However, this Enlightenment-era ideal still lacks an accounting method, which is problematic because it is the agreement on accounting standards that is the foremost feature of society, not an agreement on mutual defense, as Hobbes, Nozick and others have claimed.[11]

Civilization is the ledger and constitutes an enforceable method of recordkeeping for who owes whom, what and how much; it is recordkeeping that yields the extraordinary and unique benefit to mankind from the commonwealth idea by allowing persons to work or pay by an enforceable system of account. The ongoing process of the determination and tracking of accounts is why society is referred to as the common-*wealth*. All civilized persons agree to use force mainly and predominantly against each other to enforce the system of account; that is, the use of force is justified where any person fails to comport with the recordkeeping or methodology of accounts that has been established. Of course, this failure to comport with societal standards is the definition of a criminal. In Enlightenment-era Britain, minor property crimes were punishable by death. This is because even minor property crimes can reflect an existential threat to the system of accounts. For example, a petty thief interferes with the tracking of accounts, and a fraudster interferes with the methodology of accounts.

Many of our definitions of criminal activity, then, are for people who will not follow the accounting system that society has so painstakingly recorded and maintained. We call it "law" but what law really does is not enhance freedom or liberty, but enhance accounting. The purpose of taxation is to maintain civilization and its system of accounts against mostly internal but also occasionally external threats or even to maximize opportunities to increase wealth. The use of force by the commonwealth over matters of accounting has historically been considered legitimate to capitalize on an opportunity. For example, the British East India Company conquered India and then immediately set up an oppressive system of taxation on the local people. This was an opportunity to increase wealth by conquering and levying tax and the company took advantage of that opportunity.

The purpose of redistributive taxation is a means to protect society and its system of accounts by reducing the possibility of internal threats to the system of accounts, such as a revolt or civil unrest, by making fiscal transfers to aggrieved or disadvantaged persons. As this section goes on to explain, redistributive taxation is not intended to improve the welfare of the citizenry, although that may be a side effect if it increases the productive capacity of the commonwealth in some way. The idea of Rawlsian and similar liberal theories is to specify under what conditions redistributions should be made. The inherent drawback and limitation of these liberal ideals should be plainly apparent insofar as the welfare of persons is always subordinated to the system of account. Libertarianism more closely matches the objective of preserving the system of account, whereas liberalism is instead concerned with the general welfare. The system of account is not designed to increase the general welfare; in most cases, accounting methods are not needed to determine how to make a minimum distribution of "primary goods" to all persons to ensure their survival as a matter of Rawlsian theory, for example. Rawlsian theory is a clear illustration of a moral framework that requires the importation of an external standard by which to count beans to determine results. As we attempt to apply a cash-basis method of accounting for tax remittances to Rawlsian theory it turns out that workers pay the vast majority of taxes by that method and the results under Rawlsian theory are limited to the edges of the debate, and not very helpful.

Within the thinking of the Enlightenment era, the rough balancing of debits and credits was considered the essence of "justice."[12] That is, every person in determining what is just balances a debit on the one side and a credit on the other, and then tries to achieve a balance between the two. In a fair exchange, the balancing seems about right; in an unfair situation, a person is able to take advantage of a forced exchange of some sort, thereby taking more than he or she gives. As John Stuart Mill wrote, a "peculiar tax on the income of any class, not balanced by taxes on other classes, is a violation of justice, and amounts to a partial confiscation."[13] The underlying currency of exchange is usually money. The accounting for debits and credits in money between persons is the system of account of our society.

The preservation of the system of account also is reflected in the process of punishing criminals, whereby the debits and credits to the system of account are nominally restored to balance even when the criminal cannot pay in money. The delinquency to be corrected with a credit or debit is itself a social construct, just as Foucault proposed; however, it is done only for the sake of balancing the system of account.[14] For many types of crime, imprisonment can be avoided if the accused pays a fine (i.e., a credit) to "correct" or offset the offense (i.e., debit) *against the system*. Note that except in rare cases of restitution the offense to be offset by the payment of the fine is against the system and not against the victim or offended person. Significantly, imprisonment is a possible punishment when a person cannot pay a financial debt of some sort, so the person offsets the debt to the system by the means available to that person, which is a debit to freedom. The severe punishment of drug dealers also illustrates this point. Drug dealers are punished harshly not only because of the social harm caused by their product but also because they are thought to "cheat" the system by turning hefty profits outside the legitimate system of account and this alone is considered a significant crime.

Yet there are different ways to account for debits and credits. Nearly all philosophical debates about taxation entail variances in how society might practice the system of account. Contemporary philosophers fail to grasp that their choice of accounting method largely determines distributional results within society. Future philosophers might begin to count beans by using a cash-basis method of accounting which often functions as a default in accounting and is usually considered a reasonable method. Under a corresponding "cash"-based method of morality, each taxpayer measures tax payments in versus benefits payments out and does not count accruals. In this system, fairness would be measurable by netting beans paid in versus beans paid out today, with a positive (or neutral) balance considered presumptively fair and a negative balance considered presumptively unfair. The basic libertarian philosophy of taxation, then, can be restated as the belief that no person should be required to pay in while receiving nothing in exchange, currently, reflected in a "cash"-based method of morality. The idea that taxation is a type of theft is indeed a valid claim under such a "cash"-based method of morality[15]—indeed, it is how many people sensibly think about the tax system and the obligation to pay taxes to the state.

The appropriate response to the "cash"-based claim that taxation is theft is to posit an accrual that is offered in exchange for the taking of property, such that taxes are therefore not in the nature of theft. Society depends, in part, on the ability to convince participants of the value of an accrual received in exchange for the tax that has been paid, even if the accrual is merely forbearance from imprisonment. However, libertarians find that description of a continued freedom from imprisonment as the least persuasive of the possible accruals that might be offered in exchange and have written volumes in objection. Nonetheless, the accrual in the ledger is what distinguishes a taking from theft. For example, the taxpayer accrues the right to merchandise the property upon payment of the tax, or a person accrues the right to receive social benefits upon payment of tax, or a person accrues the right to marry or drive a car by payment of a fee. All that is merely to posit a change to an accrual-basis method of accounting. Only by positing this system of accruals does it become possible to make more complex Rawlsian, or even Posnerian,[16] statements about justness in the redistribution of beans and to explain why something that seems unfair might be justified as fair.

DEFERRAL OF TAXATION

In many situations, taxes are not required to be paid in cash immediately even in the event of a profit of some sort or accretion to wealth. The process of booking a future tax liability is often referred to as "deferral," meaning a delay in the requirement to pay a tax in cash. Tax lawyers often say that the bulk of their practice relates to deferring taxation for clients. Thus, even if the ultimate amount of tax to be paid remains the same, the deferral of tax into the future creates a benefit to the taxpayer because of the time value of money or the possibility that future events might offset the liability. This could occur, for example, if losses unexpectedly arise, which could be used to offset a past gain, or there is a change in the tax law. Accordingly, in tax parlance, the best situation is a "permanent deferral," when a tax is never to be paid even when a profit has been accrued.

In accounting practice, when a future tax is taken into account in the current period, then an accrual is placed on the books today. This accrual reflects the need to make a cash tax payment at some point in the future. The bulk of tax-planning activity for large firms relates to this process of accounting for the possibility of paying taxes in the future. Thus, reducing today's cash outlay is not really what most tax practice entails; in accounting terms, the discussion of cash payments today is referred to merely as "cash taxes" and is only part of any tax analysis that must also consider accruals. In some cases, the requirement to pay taxes in the future is certain, but more often it is uncertain, and this is indeed referred to as an "uncertain tax position." The accounting standards for recording future tax payments on these uncertain tax positions is one of the most important practical issues for tax lawyers and accountants.

If moral philosophy were practically relevant to taxation, such alternate accounting practices would need to be explicitly taken into account within the moral framework. Any discussion of moral philosophy with respect to taxation that does not consider these matters is incomplete and might draw incorrect conclusions. Therefore, one aspect of fairness with respect to taxation is defer-ral, because deferral is perhaps the most important issue in all of taxation and tax policy. A taxpayer who is able to defer taxation is more likely to consider a tax system fair, whereas taxpayer who is always required to pay taxes currently in cash is more likely to consider the system unfair. In the tax system as it stands, labor income is always taxed currently and by cash withholding, whereas cap-ital income is automatically deferred until an asset is sold. This feature of the tax system has major implications for the moral philosophy of taxation applied thereto.

PROPERTY RIGHTS AS ACCRUALS

The property rights that Nozick and others see as central to libertarianism can be coherently understood as accruals to receive future payments entered into the ledger (i.e., an entry that a person is to be paid some amount in the future). Society maintains a system of property to determine who should pay whom, who should work for whom and so on. Taxation of property, then, interferes with the ledger, which records all the accrual rights within society. That was Nozick's primary concern—to not enforce these property rights to any degree is to deny the basis of the commonwealth. Likewise, for Epstein, to change the rank-ordering of persons in property rights by redistributive taxation is also to violate the ledger. Because the system of accounts is established to track accruals, the only way to pay for something is to adjust an accrual.

In the system of accounts, property rights represent only a collection of future accruals, not a tangible thing such as cash; the initial confusion is to say that property rights are equivalent to cash (or other tangible things) under a cash-basis method of accounting. Rather, under an accrual-basis method of accounting, any property right has value in the particular system of account for society. Absent problems of relative distribution of property rights, any reduction in accrual that is thought to increase the total value of all accruals is desirable. That is to say, the commonwealth is set up both to establish and to keep records and also to undertake projects thought necessary or desirable for the common benefit, which subsequently are reflected in a net increase in accruals. Therefore, the proper justification for the taxation of property rights is that a reduction in accrual will increase accruals somewhere else by a greater degree. Societies can differ on whether a project increases overall accruals by applying different standards for which accruals are to be counted in the system of account.

Any reduction in accrual forced on a person with a property right by taxation would be considered an appropriate adjustment to the ledger if the overall value of all accruals thus increases by the productivity of the project. For example, the building of a canal or road would reduce an accrual from property when the initial tax is levied, but many other accruals would increase after successful completion of the canal or road. In comparison, an inefficient project may not have created any efficiency gain to society, but it still created an accrual that counted within the system of accounts in force at the time. However, any society that does not undertake projects at all will not continue for very long, because any temporary interference with the accrual from property rights established in the system of account will not be offset by increases to accrual from productivity; thus, society will be abandoned as soon as it appears that the accruals are (even temporarily) worthless. Infrastructure and other permanent improvements reduce the likelihood that property rights related to that society might be seen as completely worthless.

The currency used by a society is itself an accrual or promise to pay. The debasement of currency, such as that occurred in the Roman Empire at various times, represent an existential threat to society because the debasement reduces the accrual value of the currency that undermines directly the system of account. Furthermore, a society that makes more productive investments will increase its overall accruals of property rights and therefore flourish. This is by no means a guarantee of long-term success, as many factors could interfere with the permanent system of accruals, including natural disasters, changing weather, invasion or plague. However, when investments increase productivity, this increases the gross value of all the accruals. For this reason, taxes can be linked to and justified directly according to the project to which they relate. This system of a type of "direct budgeting" of cost to project is the most basic libertarian justification for taxation. For example, a football stadium might be constructed with the proceeds of a hotel tax, where the value of all nearby hotels will increase when the stadium is completed. However, the owner of the football team can capture a significant portion of the accruals apart from those that were directly budgeted to the project, paid for by reducing accruals to someone else. Persons who complain about paying the tax to increase an accrual to someone else are often objecting to the direct budgeting method. The significance of this illustration is that the method of accounting for all accruals justifies productive investment, which often determines who holds the most property rights in society.

PRODUCTIVE WORK IN LIBERTARIANISM

This leads to another tenet of libertarian ideology, derived from John Locke, which is that productive work relates to the origin of property rights in society. Productive work is also important to the system of account where it is a factor of production. As Cockfield explained:

> In Locke's view, the overriding consideration attaching private property to the philosophical vision of the self is the transformation of the property by the individual's labor, adding value to it and making it more productive in character. As such, the individual has a right to the transformed property or to trade the property for money because the property now consists of "his own person." Locke thus emphasizes the relationship between an individual's productive behavior and the consequences of this behavior, which are critical aspects of individual liberty.[17]

Under any system of accounting, the rights of persons depend on their relation to accounts. If work increases account balances by increasing production, then persons who work have a direct influence on accounts, whereas persons who do not work have no influence or only an indirect influence. Therefore, workers have more default rights in an accounting system than nonworkers because they have a greater ability to influence accounts. This is why libertarian theory refers directly to productive work. So, where Nozick says that wage taxation is a type of forced labor, this is a complaint that persons who work do not receive anything in return for their productive work. Again, this libertarian view is accurate from the perspective of a cash-basis method of accounting but not an accrual-basis method of accounting. Nozick is correct that work is normally performed pursuant to which an accrual is initially received in return, and that wage taxes directly reduce any payment before it is even received by the worker. So, the accrual is made to the worker for the work performed and then reduced by taxation. If the wage tax is for social insurance, the worker then receives an accrual credit within the social insurance system for the reduction of wages. The wage tax is offset by nominal accrual of some kind, even forbearance from imprisonment. This means that the worker got some type of accrual in exchange for work.

The system of account can offer only the possibility of an accrual as an exchange, although by the counting of actual beans represented in the accruals, moral philosophers may attempt to show that affairs of state are substantively fair or unfair in specific contexts. Other scholars have thereby criticized libertarian theory on the grounds of undue accumulation of property rights. The concern is that accumulations might interfere with incentives to work. However, the Enlightenment-era idea of the commonwealth implies a human tendency toward wealth accumulation that persists in modern society. This seems a valid approach even though the tendency of humans to engage in wealth accumulation may not be universal to all societies; if the tendency toward wealth accumulation is merely a local phenomenon limited to present-day capitalism, then this tendency could be developed as a critique of Enlightenment thought.

Next, to discuss redistributive taxation, it is necessary first to introduce different types of accounts—current accounts and noncurrent accounts—and to explain why redistributive taxes are levied in a system of accounts. The accounts that society is most concerned with are current accounts, or the day-to-day transfers between persons, but especially between workers and employers. So, a current account between worker and employer is, for example, the agreement to pay the worker enough money to be able to acquire food, housing and other necessities to survive currently and thereby to continue to work. Current accounts are central to business accounting. For example, if a supplier invoice is not paid, then the necessary supplies don't come in to make the end product and the business comes to a halt immediately—not a month from now, but immediately. The primary danger is that the system of current accounts might collapse and workers stop working.

In contrast, noncurrent accounts refer to longer-term promises to pay that also have the potential to stop business, but it would take longer for them to do so. Examples are corporate securities, Treasury bonds and so forth. The general rule is that in terms of payment priority, current accounts come first, and then noncurrent accounts. Accordingly, wage accruals should be understood as a type of current account, whereas property rights are a type of noncurrent account. This means that if society had to choose between levying a confisca-tory tax on a wage payment versus a property right, then confiscatory taxes on wage accruals are a more immediate threat to the system of account. Therefore, redistributive taxes might be levied in order to prevent systemic problems by increasing current welfare in society. This could be necessary if, for example, the amount of wage accruals is insufficient to provide for the needs of workers. If the system allows for extremely low wages, then redistributive taxation could be necessary to offset problems in the current accounts of low-income workers.

LIBERTARIANISM AND ACCOUNTING METHODS

Because productive work is related to a system of account designed to increase accruals for the commonwealth, it is possible to readily distinguish libertarianism from liberalism, economics, Marxist economics and contempo-rary libertarianism. This effort to distinguish the respective fields of analysis based on the treatment of productive work within the system of accounts is necessary because literature in the philosophy of taxation has blended concepts of liberty and efficiency.[18]

Libertarianism and liberalism

Rawlsian liberalism effectively rejects the libertarian idea that the potential for productive work yields special rights to workers beyond the value of accruals received in return. As explained earlier, some versions of libertarian theory, especially variants of Hobbesian analysis, are concerned explicitly with the common defense. Liberalism, however, does not broach this idea, or at least not to the same degree. In any case, since Rawls is not concerned with production or defense as an end in itself, but rather merely welfare in its broad sense, redistributions could occur by liberal principles via the tax system; these are not desirable under libertarianism.[19]

The freedom to be free from taxation is not a "basic liberty" in the Rawlsian framework.[20] This failure to include tax freedom in the respective basic freedoms of Rawlsian liberalism is also true under a libertarian system of accounts, but solely in reference to the taxation of property rights. That is, noncurrent accruals reflected in property rights may be taxed in an attempt to increase the net noncurrent accruals from property. This is axiomatic to any definition of a commonwealth. However, in libertarianism, productive work entails special rights because it tends to increase the value of all accruals on a current basis. One of these rights (as Nozick and Locke propose in so many words) is the nontaxation of current accruals derived from work. The idea is that taxing current accounts is likely to decrease productivity by interfering with wage accruals necessary to production. For example, if wages are set at levels just high enough for workers to cover living expenses, then wage taxes would prevent productive work, thus harming the system of accounts even in the event of an offsetting accrual. Therefore, the freedom to be free from wage taxation (at least with subsistence levels of wages) is a "basic liberty" under libertarianism. As explained in detail by Arthur Cockfield, "Due to the adverse impact of both income and consumption taxes on laboring activity, the ideal Lockean tax would presumably involve neither of these taxes. Instead, the ideal Lockean tax would tax only those activities that have nothing to do with an individual's productive behavior."[21]

The "primary good" that Rawls describes is essentially equivalent to the maintenance of current welfare in accounting terms but as applied to all persons, not just workers. The Rawlsian idea of the "primary good" is reflected in the idea of current welfare. That is, at minimum, workers should be paid enough after taxes to survive in the current period in order to perform the work in the current period. Rawlsian theory differs in that resources could be redistributed even to persons who are not currently working or may not be able to work. Libertarians, if pushed, could not agree with redistribution to persons who lack the capacity to work, as this is an ideal belonging solely to common welfare. The distinction between workers' welfare and the welfare of all persons is a primary difference between libertarianism and liberalism.

Liberalism's "difference principle" does not exist in a system of accounts. As a matter of accounting, there is no "difference principle," which is as Edgren says "the [re]distribution of income and wealth [are] permitted [...] to increase the well-being of the worst off representative person."[22] The accumulation of wealth is the purpose of the commonwealth, so the idea of taking action regarding the lowest members of society is anathema to the system. Nonetheless, a similar concept could be incorporated by changing the period of account to a longer-term perspective. That is, in financial accounting today, earnings are reported on a quarterly basis, which is generally agreed to be a short-term measure. Business managers are usually paid, in part, based on financial results. This means that financials are often reported to maximize short-term results at the expense of long-term gains. For example, a company may, to the extent possible under the accounting rules, accelerate income or decelerate costs within the current quarter. This has the effect of pushing an offsetting item into a later period. To some extent, the difference principle entails a short-term perspective if there is any wastage of workers (or spoilage of property). If any workers are left to starve, or if their skills deteriorate because of long periods of unemployment, then it might be efficient to apply a "difference principle" to maintain the workforce in the short term, even with an added cost. That cost might then be offset over the long term. This long-term view within the system of account might approximates the difference principle posited by Rawls.

In summary, Rawlsian liberalism incorporated into Enlightenment-era thought various accruals toward the general welfare. The concepts of the primary good and the difference principle were proposed changes to the system of account applied by society to account for the general welfare.

LIBERTARIANISM VERSUS ECONOMICS

Libertarianism should be interpreted as generally opposed to high tax on labor in the form of any taxes levied on productive work. Lock's libertarian view as applied to taxation is that taxes on labor reduce the productivity of labor by reducing incentives to freely contract out one's own labor. Of course, that interpretation is not reflective of the special version of libertarianism called "contemporary libertarianism." Adherents to this special version of libertarianism often favor the elimination of taxes on capital or inheritance taxes. The focus in libertarianism on productive work also distinguishes it from economic theory. Economic theory reverses the Lockean understanding of productivity to say that it is inevitable that labor will bear the incidence of taxation; therefore, it is more efficient that taxes be levied directly on labor. The idea of economics is that taxes on capital reduce the productivity of capital in each jurisdiction to some degree.

The relevant question here is whether the method of accounting for labor or capital costs might change the incentives described in libertarian or economic theory. As I have explained elsewhere, the given method of accounting does change the incentives within a system of income taxation.[23] Deductions for capital investment are often accelerated under an income tax system. Therefore, any company that makes capital investment into a local jurisdiction gets a tax benefit in the form of accelerated depreciation deductions. Therefore, once a business becomes profitable in any jurisdiction, cash taxes can be reduced from capital investment. The gist of economic theory applies to the separate situation of determining whether a business might be expected to make a first investment into a location based on the tax rate that might accrue on future profits; basically, economic theory predicts that a lower tax rate means greater business profits and investments. However, the former libertarian description appears to be the more relevant description of capital investment, as large firms that are already profitable in many countries need to decide where to place the bulk of available investment capital. This analysis could help explain why countries with relatively higher tax rates seem to nearly always experience higher rates of capital investment and higher rates of economic growth, as compared to countries with lower tax rates.

LIBERTARIANISM VERSUS MARXIST ECONOMICS

Given the focus on productive work, a nominal similarity seems to exist between Lockean libertarian theory and Marxist economics, which has not been sufficiently explored in the literature. Modern-day scholars seem reluctant to describe libertarianism in terms of productive work for fear of confusion with Marxism. However, with an understanding premised on the system of account, there should be no danger of confusion. Marxist theory posits work as an end in itself, as work allows for the worker's self-realization. The idea is that productive activity is the essence of human activity, and capitalism alienates mankind from that essence. Marxism posits a type of worker's utopia in that all persons in society are given the opportunity to achieve self-realization through work under conditions of collective property rights.

A parallel version of a libertarian utopia would be if the Lockean ideal of productive work could be combined with the Jeffersonian ideal of individual property ownership. The goal in this utopia would be to combine productive work with property ownership, even to a small degree, and through that combination society is thought to flourish. The parallel essence of mankind in the libertarian utopia is to obtain self-realization by translating productive work into property rights, comprising a stake in wealth, the tracking of which is made possible by the commonwealth. The Jeffersonian ideal is in some ways similar to Nozick's libertarian idea of the "minimum state," where the state is set at the minimum conditions necessary to allow for the small property owner utopia. Each independent stakeholder is further granted an equal voice in the government of the "minimum state." Some of the ideals of the libertarian utopia continues to a large extent in the modern-day United States, where small business activity is lionized and viewed as a desirable engine of economic growth—that is, toward the expansion of the commonwealth.

The literature has distinguished Marxism from libertarianism on the grounds that Nozick and others have a merely "bourgeois" philosophy, which is incorrect. The Lockean or Jeffersonian small stakeholder is not bourgeois; many successful small business owners display almost no appetite for consumption. Rather, the productive activity of small business owners seems to relate to the production of wealth as a human activity, of which productive work is one limited component. A system of account is necessary to that endeavor in order to track what each individual has achieved in terms of wealth accumulation;[24] thus, the system of account becomes the measurement criteria for the human activity of wealth creation. In addition, small business owners often do not measure inheritance of wealth as a success equivalent to the founding or operation of a business. Accordingly, a legitimate philosophical question is whether the system of account should be modified to discount the value of inherited wealth in the commonwealth and recognize instead only the value of the production of wealth. The obvious means to recognize wealth production over wealth inheritance would be to levy a significant inheritance tax. The significant point here is that libertarianism is consistent with inheritance taxes, notwithstanding that contemporary libertarianism has taken the view that capital taxes are most evil or that all taxes are equally evil.[25]

REDISTRIBUTIVE TAXATION AND LIBERTARIANISM

Many philosophical discussions of tax revolve around private property rights. These concerns have been distilled logically to what is referred to as the "libertarian challenge" to taxation.[26] As a simple backdrop, economic theory is concerned with efficiency, and philosophy with rightness. Of course, economists think that efficiency actually is rightness, and there has accordingly been some blending of concepts between philosophy and economics in the context of taxation. The basic idea of rightness for the libertarian challenge is that taxes always reduce private property, which must be a violation of first principles of rightness. Progressive taxation is especially problematic because it changes the "rank order" of persons in property holdings, which is the greatest wrong for libertarians.[27]

The libertarian challenge is extremely important because it constitutes the greatest obfuscation in all of tax theory. The trouble is this: Wealth accumulations have become so large that fortunes cannot be readily converted from fiat money (e.g., money held in bank accounts) into tangible private property. If the wealthy were to attempt to take fiat money and translate electronic bank account entries into property, then the prices of property would dramatically increase, making this conversion impossible in practical terms, at least. Vast fortunes serve only as a status symbol to rank order persons according to accumulated money and holdings, similar to the Enlightenment era, when the wealthy rank-ordered themselves by acreage and slave holdings. Therefore, the taxation of money is not automatically a taking of private property, as assumed by the libertarian challenge. The premise that taxation reduces private property is simply incorrect. To the wealthy, the only thing that matters is their ranking in comparison to other wealthy person, and absolutely not what their accumulated hoards of money could actually buy. In fact, redistributive taxes could be designed for levy on accumulated hoards of money without changing the rank order of wealthy persons vis-à-vis one another. Hence, the proceeds of redistributive taxation could be employed to make people better off without making any person worse off, a roughly Pareto-optimal result.

LIBERTARIANISM VERSUS CONTEMPORARY LIBERTARIANISM

A significant difference has arisen between libertarianism in its classical sense, often referring to the writings of John Locke, and contemporary libertarianism, referring to a political ideology in the United States associated with a small or diminished role of the federal government and low taxes, especially on capital and inheritance. Other nontax ideals are also associated with contemporary libertarianism, such as the right to bear arms and the legalization of marijuana. Contemporary libertarianism incorporates several ideals that are new and relevant to taxation; they are discussed here in the context of the system of account.

EACH AS HIS OR HER OWN SOVEREIGN

The first idea of "contemporary libertarianism" that distinguishes it from classical or other versions of libertarianism is that each person functions essentially as his or her own sovereign. Epstein famously described his version of libertarianism in a "Lockean world" where the citizen was above the sovereign as follows: "Taxation is the power to coerce other individuals to surrender their property without their consent. In a world—a Lockean world—in which liberty is regarded as a good and coercion an evil, then taxation authorizes the sovereign to commit acts of aggression against the very citizens it is supposed to protect [...] the citizen is made the servant instead of the master of the sovereign."[28] Although it is not clear whether a citizen above a sovereign would reserve the right to use force, other versions of contemporary libertarianism advance the idea that the person reserves the right to bear arms and to use force, as a sovereign would. As explained earlier, the defining feature of civilization, though, is not the use of force but the preservation of the system of accounts. A sovereign is not entitled to vary the system of accounts under the terms of a constitution; indeed, this is the primary reason for having a constitution or constitutional monarchy. However, the fundamental agreement of a commonwealth is that the system of account should be standardized and enforceable by the state. Each person should therefore not feel the need to individually enforce the system of account. A better solution for libertarians would be to simply not deal with outsiders or criminals who do not follow the established rules. Notably, however, the term "railroading" has entered the nomenclature in the United States to refer to the government or large business encroaching on the rights of small stakeholders. However, the possibility that the strong prey on the weak is foremost a legal issue where laws should be enforced to better protect the accounts of small stakeholders, and not a problem with the actual system of accounts in the commonwealth.

If each individual were granted the right to use force to maintain the system of accounts in order to defeat problems with coercion, this would create a potential problem because force could be used to take advantage in the system. That is, a legitimate or illegitimate dispute might arise, and the libertarian-as-sovereign could use force to violate the system of account. The counter to the "each is his or her own sovereign" ideal is, therefore, that the higher the number of persons who have the potential to use force, the greater the likelihood that force will be used. Accordingly, the classical libertarian view *should* be that each person should not be entitled to use force to enforce the system of account; in situations where persons are not reliable enough to follow the system of account, libertarians should avoid dealing with those persons to the extent possible or should deal with them only on a cash basis.

The appropriate response to a contemporary libertarian rightfully concerned about coercion through the tax system is that of course a system of account is coercive and reduces liberty. But by adding in an accrual for the coercion, we debit liberty on the one side and credit it on the other, and this results in a net gain to liberty through the commonwealth. The dispute over coercion is how to do the crediting of liberty to the taxpayer. All Enlightenment-era ideals begin by presuming the potential to both debit and credit, so we must do the crediting and can debate only how it is to be done.

ALL TAXES ARE EQUALLY EVIL

The opposition to all forms of taxation in contemporary libertarianism may be an attempt to limit the size of government by eliminating its funding. In the libertarian philosophy of Nozick, the justification for a "minimal state" was provided along these lines. However, this varies from classical libertarianism in that justice is determined by the counting of debits (tax payments in) and credits (benefit payments out) by each individual. This means that a classical libertarian would tolerate a larger state if the overall balancing of debits and credits from the state led to a net increase in allocable accruals or cash payments under an agreed method of accounting. The difference in viewpoint about tax policy, therefore, is merely in the accounting for accruals of various sorts. Put simply, a contemporary libertarian who asserts that all taxes are equally evil is essentially obtuse as to how different types of accruals can benefit the welfare of individuals and society, and which system of accounts can be used to measure those benefits.

The appropriate classical libertarian response to the "all taxes are equally evil" idea is that in the measurement of accruals, various taxes should be expected to have varying effects, depending on the context. For example, some types of taxes should be expected to immediately end the commonwealth, as illustrated in Britain, where the conservative government of Margaret Thatcher attempted to implement a head tax (or capitation tax) rather than an income tax, which led to riots and chaos. This also can be illustrated more broadly by this example: If a complete tax on all wage accruals was implemented, labor should be expected to completely cease if persons would not agree to work without current wages; society would immediately collapse, and nearly all accruals would become worthless. The more difficult situation arises when the tax type creates an incentive that may be expected to impact the system of accruals favorably or unfavorably. Persons may disagree as to what tax types may have which effect. As explained throughout, this disagreement is premised largely on differences in the choice of the methodology of account. The differences relate to counting accruals in different ways, yet the goal of the commonwealth that accruals be increased on an aggregate by the tax system is not in dispute. Therefore, when placed in context, all taxes are not equally evil, and neither are they equally beneficial.

UTILITARIANISM

Utilitarianism is helpful to accounting because it provides a means for each individual person to measure or count welfare to their own person. Pleasure or pain is measured in utiles. By counting utiles related to various events, each person can create a standard for measurement and implement an individualized system of account. But the utile measures are not interchangeable between persons. This means, for example, that if a person offers to exchange a loaf of bread with another person for two utiles worth of something else, the person with the bread has no basis to judge whether that exchange is fair. Therefore, to judge fairness, using the system of account as an interpersonal means to measure debits and credits between persons is required. Currency is often used as the medium of account to resolve this problem; however, labor is often exchanged for currency on the basis of hours, and many other in-kind mediums of exchange are posited within accounting methods for cost. Richard Posner's wealth maximization standard of utilitarianism is helpful as a form of applied utilitarianism, because wealth is taken to be exchangeable between persons, whereas standard utility is not. This means that money can be used as a proxy for utility to each individual, often referred to as an individual welfare function. Since money is often applied as the medium within the system of account, the idea that money can often be used as a proxy for utility to each individual is already assumed within the standard accounting method.

There are limits, though, to the use of money as a proxy for utility (or welfare) that are also important to recognize in setting tax policy on the basis of welfare. First, the dead do not have utility, so money works as a proxy for utility only during life. Second, money may have diminishing returns to scale, so at some point of accumulation, any incremental gains in money do not add very much to utility. Third, and of particular significance to accounting method, money cannot always be traded into property. Money represents in accounting terms both cash, which is a type of current asset (an asset expected to be used in some way), and wealth (with money representing a tracking of accruals in the form of property rights). These are not the same.

CONCLUSION: THE MISSING PHILOSOPHICAL INQUIRY ON THE FAIRNESS OF HIGH TAX RATES ON PRODUCTIVE WORK

Nearly all taxes on productive work are levied on a cash basis, where taxes are withheld from the worker's paycheck before he or she receives the funds; the taxation of work occurs immediately and is almost never deferred except for funds set aside for retirement, such as in a 401(k) account. The taxation of productive work comprised roughly 82 percent of the overall revenue base in the United States. The effective rate on labor approaches or exceeds 50 percent in most OECD (Organisation for Economic Co-operation and Development) countries, which is comparatively higher than the rate of tax on investment income or corporate income by a wide margin. In comparison, taxes on capital are delayed, as there is automatic deferral until a recognition event occurs. Tax receipts from capital gains are so low in the United States that during economic downturns the IRS does not release data on the actual amount collected until years after the fact.

A surprising aspect of philosophical writings on the fairness of the tax system is that moral philosophers have not addressed the fairness of high rates of tax levied on productive work. This may be a result of the unique method of accounting within various strains of moral philosophy. The approach is to always posit the possibility of future benefits that workers get in exchange for the tax remittance paid in cash today. Commentators often posit that workers get more benefits than they pay in taxes; thus, they have in mind a net gain to workers based on a posited high accrual of future benefits. However, this offset methodology is not applied in any other context of tax policy. At minimum, the various standards of moral philosophy applied to taxation, especially standards premised in Enlightenment-era thought, which do not address the issue of the fairness of the heavy taxation of productive work, are not "Lockean" and are misleading applications of libertarianism.

NOTES

1 See Richard A. Epstein, *One Step Beyond Nozick's Minimal State: The Role of Forced Exchanges in Political Theory*, 22:1 Soc. Phil & Pol'y 286, 292 (2005) ("But even here Nozick does not quite want to allow taxation into the system, even on a proportional basis, which distinguishes his position from that of other classical thinkers such as John Locke, Adam Smith, and Friedrich von Hayek, all of whom gravitate in that direction."), citing John Locke, Second Treatise, in *Two Treatises of Government*, ed. P. Laslett, 363 (Cambridge: Cambridge University Press, 1989); Adam Smith, *The Wealth of Nations* (New York: Modern Library, 1937); Friedrich A. Hayek, *The Constitution of Liberty* (Chicago, IL: University of Chicago Press, 1960), at 314.

2 Richard A. Epstein, *Taxation with Representation: Or, the Libertarian Dilemma*, 18 Can. J.L. & Juris. 7, 12 (2005) ("Yet once it is recognized that the provision of these public goods [...] counts as an important function of taxation, Nozick's objections to taxation as a system of forced labor fall apart.").

3 John Rawls, *Political Liberalism* (New York: Columbia University Press, 1986); see also John Rawls, *A Theory of Justice* (Cambridge: Harvard University Press, 1971).

4 Jürgen Habermas, Richard Rorty's Pragmatic Turn, in *Rorty and His Critics* (Malden, MA: Blackwell, 2000), at 49 ("In the lifeworld actors depend on behavior certainties. They have to cope with a world presumed to be objective, and, for this reason, operate with the distinction between believing and knowing. There is a practical necessity to rely intuitively on what is unconditionally held to be true.").

5 See, e.g., Epstein, *One Step Beyond Nozick's Minimal State*, at 290 ("For example, Nozick's view would prevent the state from supplying what have been commonly termed public goods—namely, those goods (such as streetlights and national defense) that must be supplied to all members of a community if they are to be supplied to any individual member. This position can easily result in situations in which everyone is worse off in a world without taxation than they would be in a world with a well-designed system.").

6 See L. Murphy & T. Nagel, *The Myth of Ownership: Taxes and Justice* (Oxford: Oxford University Press, 2002).

7 See Congressional Budget Office, *Effective Tax Rates for Low- and Moderate-Income Workers*, www.cbo.gov/sites/default/files/cbofiles/attachments/11-15-2012-MarginalTax Rates.pdf. Accessed Nov. 10, 2019.

8 Internal Revenue Code, § 1031 et seq.

9 Richard A. Epstein, *Taxation in a Lockean World*, 4:1 Soc. Phil. & Pol. 64–5 (1986).

10 Vilfredo Pareto, *Manual of Political Economy*, ed. Montesano, Zanni, Bruni, Chipman and McLure (Oxford: Oxford University Press, [1906] 2014); Epstein, *Taxation with Representation*, at 7 ("The first point to note is that virtually any tax system will leave just about everyone (the practical standard for Pareto superiority) better off than they are in the state of nature. Someone has to decide which of these systems is better [...] In addition, the problem becomes more difficult because certain collective decisions have negative utility for some individuals and positive utility for others, without any opportunity to partition the two sets.").

11 Thomas Hobbes, *Leviathan: Or the Matter, Forme, and Power of a Common-Wealth Ecclesiastical and Civil*, ed. Waller (Cambridge: Cambridge University Press, [1651] 1904).

12 James S. Coleman, Boris Frankel & Derek L. Phillips, *Robert Nozick's Anarchy, State, and Utopia*, 3:3 Theory & Soc. 437, 439 (1976) ("Nozick points out that any end-result conception of distributive justice, if embodied in law, gives each citizen an enforceable claim to some portion of the total social product, regardless of who currently holds that product or how they came to hold it.").

13 B. Clark & J. Elliott, *John Stuart Mill's Theory of Justice*, 59:4 Rev. Soc. Econ. 467 (2001), citing John Stuart Mill, *Collected Works of John Stuart Mill*, ed. J. M. Robson (Toronto: University of Toronto Press; London: Routledge and Keegan Paul, 1963–1991); John Stuart Mill, *On Liberty*, 2nd edn. (London: Parker, 1859).

14 Michel Foucault, *Discipline and Punish: The Birth of the Prison*, tr. Sheridan (New York: Second Vintage Books Edition, 1977, 1995); Bret N. Bogenschneider, *Foucault and Tax Jurisprudence: On the Creation of a "Delinquent" Class of Taxpayer*, 8 Wash. U. Juris. Rev. 59 (2015).

15 M. Rothbard, *The Myth of Neutral Taxation*, Cato J. 66 (1981): "It is true that if taxation were voluntary and the government akin to a business firm, the government would be neutral to the market. We contend here, however, that the model of government is akin, not to the business firm, but to the criminal organization, and indeed that the State is the organization of robbery systematized and writ large."

16 Richard Posner, *Utilitarianism, Economics, and Legal Theory*, 8 J. Legal Stud. 103 (1979); but see Ronald Dworkin, *Is Wealth a Value?* 9 J. Legal Stud. 191 (1980); see also Richard A. Posner, *Wealth Maximization Revisited*, 2 Notre Dame J. Law, Ethics & Pub. Pol'y 85 (1985).

17 Arthur Cockfield, *Income Taxes and Individual Liberty: A Lockean Perspective on Radical Consumption Tax Reform*, 46 S. DAK. L. REV. 8, 29 (2001).

18 See, e.g., Geoffrey P. Miller, *Economic Efficiency and the Lockean Proviso*, 10 HARV. J.L. & PUB. POL'Y 401, 410 (1987) ("The effect of the Proviso is to require that the transfers of excess property (that is, property in excess of the appropriator's pro rata share) out of the commons into private hands is permitted if the state of affairs resulting from the transfer is pareto-superior to that which subsisted before. Transfers will be permitted if they result in at least one person being made better off and no one being made worse off than he or she was before. Transfers that are ruled out by the Proviso are those that are pareto-inferior, in that even though the appropriator may be better off as a consequence of his or her action, others will be worse off.").

19 James Repetti & Paul McDaniel, *Horizontal and Vertical Equity: The Musgrave/Kaplow Exchange*, 10 FLA. TAX REV. 607 (1993), at 610 ("In the context of taxation, Rawls concluded that the best tax system for his theory of justice may be a flat tax rate on consumption. By design, a tax on consumption only exempts capital income from tax and capital income is concentrated in the upper income levels.").

20 John Edgren, *On the Relevance of John Rawls's Theory of Justice to Welfare Economics*, 53:3 REV. SOC. ECON. 343 (1995), citing Rawls, *A Theory of Justice* (1971), at 343 ("The basic liberties are political liberty, freedom of speech and assembly, liberty of conscience and freedom of thought, freedom of the person, the right to own property, freedom from arbitrary arrest and seizure.").

21 Cockfield, *Income Taxes and Individual Liberty*, at 30.

22 Edgren, *On the Relevance of John Rawls's Theory of Justice to Welfare Economics*, at 343.

23 Bret N. Bogenschneider, *The Tax Paradox of Capital Investment*, 33:1 J. TAX'N INV. 59 (2015).

24 Locke, Second Treatise, 318–19 ("And indeed it was a foolish thing, as well as dishonest, to hoard up more than he could make use of.").

25 F. Chodorov, *The Income Tax: Root of All Evil.* (New York: Devin-Adair; Ludwig von Mises Institute, [1954] 2002).

26 Daniel Attas, *Fragmenting Property*, 25 LAW & PHIL. 119–49 (2006); but see Bret N. Bogenschneider, *A Challenge to the Libertarian Challenge*, 31 J. JURIS. 9 (2017).

27 Richard A. Epstein, *Taxation in a Lockean World*, 4:1 SOC. PHIL. & POL. 49 (1986). Several other scholars have argued that tax equity can be identified in terms of rank ordering reversals caused by the tax system. A. B. Atkinson, Horizontal Equity and the Distribution of the Tax Burden, in *The Economics of Taxation*, ed. Aaron & Boskin (Washington, DC: Brookings Institute, 1980); Robert Plotnick, *A Measure of Horizontal Inequity*, 63 REV. ECON. & STAT. 283 (1981).

28 Epstein, *Taxation in a Lockean World*, at 49.

CHAPTER 5

WAGE TAXES DO HAVE
SOCIAL COSTS

Chapter Summary: *Taxes levied on workers entail a social cost similar to other types of taxes. The social costs of wage taxation reflect the negative impact of taxation to the person who is required to pay the tax. Workers channel capital into investments that generate a social gain (or investment return) to society, such as children or their own health, so increasing taxes on workers should be expected to yield a reduction in social outcomes to workers. For example, as the relative taxation of workers in the United States increased, obesity rates also increased. Any social costs with respect to worker taxation have never been taken into account as a matter of economic theory, even though social costs are taken into account with respect to the taxation of the wealthy and large corporations. Furthermore, contrary to statements by other prominent tax scholars, workers largely fund their own social benefit programs through wage withholding. The wealthy do not fund the so-called welfare state by making transfer payments to the working poor through government programs—this idea is nonsense and cannot be used as the premise of tax policy. Any coherent description of tax policy requires an accounting method that reflects that workers pay most of the taxes now and should be expected to pay the taxes into the future. Accounting methods that posit that the wealthy will pay significant taxes in the future are unrealistic because the wealthy do not fund the budget through taxes today. The overall tax rates in the United States are heavily regressive; the top quintile of earners pay an effective tax rate that is roughly one-third that paid by those with lower income. Thomas Piketty's estimate of income inequality is vastly understated because the data set used taxable income from tax returns and did not take into account holding gains in capital assets (as separately tracked by the Federal Reserve). A primary source of inequality is actually the lower effective tax rates paid by the wealthy in comparison to other persons.*

The wealthy and the ruling classes and nobility have always believed, like Leona Helmsley, that workers are inferior and expendable, and that there is nothing valuable to society in workers. Workers are essentially cogs. The collective efforts of the working class in laboring and raising their families have no more importance to society than ants on an anthill. Because of this, tax scholarship justifies that the workers should and must pay the taxes in society no matter what. Economic theorists say that it is supposedly efficient for the workers to pay the taxes no matter what and no matter how much evidence may exist that taxes are harmful to working people. Nonetheless, if you read the theory on taxation presented in academic literature described as libertarian, conservative or even philosophically liberal, you will find that in nearly all cases, the intended audience is the wealthy as a class, and the research always concludes that it is right, fair, efficient, or inevitable that workers pay the taxes and not the wealthy.

Although it may seem obvious to the readers of this book that wage taxes are harmful to the persons required to pay those taxes, this idea is considered audacious by most economists. The idea that workers should matter in the design of tax policy, in fact, challenges nearly all of the applied economic doctrine used to formulate tax policy. If such a radical idea were incorporated into tax policy design, it would change or even reverse the results of most economic modeling calling for tax cuts for large corporations and tax increases for workers, and this is true even if we left all the other variables in the models untouched. In other words, one only needs to know how an economist feels about tax incidence to know what recommendation they will make on tax policy—that is, tax the workers—and there is no empirical data that would potentially change that recommendation. Usually absolute beliefs are reserved for religion, but the reader should see at this point that absolute beliefs are also predominant in taxation and tax policy and these beliefs are really fixed and cannot be changed by the creation or offering of evidence.

Yet, the idea that workers matter to tax policy only seems outrageous to those economists immersed completely in the economic doctrine of taxation, which is far removed from the reality of modern society. Persons closer to the tax system—namely the workers and the taxpayers—immediately understand that wage taxes are harmful to working people and the negative results should be measured in the formulation of tax policy, and further, that this idea is not so audacious and is really quite reasonable, conservative, even libertarian. Accordingly, the basic premise of economic thinking on taxation is contrary to the beliefs of most working people and most taxpayers and they would find it unreasonable if it were explained to them—it must therefore remain secret, or at least, largely unknown. Hence, the title of this book; to begin to discuss tax incidence analysis is to reveal a secret of tax policy that has been hidden from America.

One thesis of this chapter is that the assertion that wage taxes have social costs is plainly true based on even a cursory review of the available evidence, and views to the contrary represent an unrealistic premise of an economic model. Indeed, the formulation of an economic model of tax incidence is just the beginning and not the end of tax policy analysis. The term "tax incidence" refers to who is assumed to bear the burden of taxation and will be further explained below. Choice of model is only the beginning of analysis because that choice of model is an inductive process even if the persons making the choices are absolutely convinced of the superiority of their own cognitive abilities—as economists surely are. It is appropriate to counter this choice in scientific terms by pointing out that the inductive choice of economic model might be wrong, and probably is wrong, at least if we look at any empirical evidence, so we need to check then if the model corresponds to the actual. In other words, we need to determine whether wage taxes do, or do not, have social costs. This is a valid and important project for tax policy. Yet, economic scholars have not yet undertaken this project of beginning to explain why wage taxes should be expected not to entail social costs. Since the project has not begun, I would say that at the very minimum the analysis of tax incidence is incomplete.

All or nearly all empirical results appear to be to the contrary of economic modeling of tax incidence, and accordingly the standard economic modeling of tax incidence is drastically incorrect. Wage taxes do have social costs, and the costs appear to be astronomical. The origin of the unrealistic approach to economic analysis of tax incidence was Thomas Malthus. He imagined that social costs to workers should be ignored as a matter of economic policy all the way back in the nineteenth century. The industrial classes of Malthus's time were eager to justify their practice of paying low wages to the working class and embraced this approach to economic policy. Malthus justified the idea by claiming that workers waste away the proceeds of work anyway so there was nothing that the capitalists could do to help save the workers from themselves, so why bother? Obviously, it would be inefficient to bother with workers that waste all capital they might acquire anyway. Centuries later, other economists, led by Arnold Harberger, imagined roughly the same idea again, but this time applied it specifically to taxation and tax policy. That model, referred to as the "small open economy model" became the basis of tax policy design used by nearly all economists today.

WHO REALLY FUNDS THE WELFARE STATE?

A significant portion of tax scholarship begins with a puzzling description of the so-called welfare state.[1] The assumption is that progressive income tax rates mean that somehow the poor are getting a net transfer benefit through the tax system; that is, a benefit that exceeds the taxes they pay into the system. Although it is possible that individual persons might be able to draw in more than they pay out in relatively rare cases, poorer workers as a whole pay in vastly more than they receive. The reason for this is briefly that the Social Security system does not have progressive rates so the wealthy tend to draw more money out than the working poor. There is also an indexed cap above which earnings are no longer subject to Social Security withholding; and second, wealthier persons tend to live longer than poor persons, which means that they draw out more benefits from the social support system.[2] Not all the reasons that the wealthy live longer are understood, but the answer is probably that they have better access to health care, they exercise more and they eat better and healthier food or some combination thereof. Accordingly, long-lived persons, many of whom are wealthy, draw out vastly disproportionate amounts from the Social Security system than their shorter-lived peers.

The one consistent truth about all tax systems around the world is that workers in the aggregate fund social welfare payments to themselves.[3] In terms of funding for the welfare state, it is workers who pay in cash today for transfer payments to others, and income taxes levied on wealthy persons are not used for this purpose, despite unsupported claims by many tax scholars. In actual practice, the worker receives a paycheck from which some amount is withheld and paid over to the government to be held in trust. That cash from withholdings is then used to fund payments to other persons, such as to retired workers and disabled persons. However, nearly all social welfare systems run at a surplus. The surplus means that workers pay in far more than is required to be paid out in present benefits. Such surplus is held by the government ostensibly until benefits need to be paid. Because of the difference in sizes of the respective generations of workers, the United States is only now approaching the novel situation in which its cash flows from the Social Security system might begin to turn negative; that is, the outflow of cash from Social Security payments exceeds the inflow of cash from withholding labor income. An open question is whether and how the federal government will fund itself during an economic crisis when it has negative rather than positive cash flows to draw on from its primary source of revenue to fund the government (i.e., Social Security withholding from worker's paychecks).

The preliminary point of accounting for tax remittance is that working persons fund Social Security benefits mainly through wage withholding. Any transfer payments that fund the welfare state derive mostly from these and other wage taxes paid by other workers. Furthermore, these transfer systems are nearly always accounted for separately from the income tax system. Social benefit systems around the world nearly always run at a surplus, and Social Security is no exception. Given the surplus of money on its balance sheet, government officials are tempted to access that money and use it today. In the United States, the federal government borrowed from the Social Security Trust Fund to provide the cash to fund the budget deficit in each year and gave back an IOU to the fund. The Social Security system currently holds mostly federal IOUs, rendering it now essentially an unfunded defined-benefit pension system.

Eventually, the federal government will become cash-flow negative. As an accounting matter, it is sometimes possible to gain insights by examining cash flows rather than contrived measures of income. Among other things, as the federal government turns cash-flow negative, the Social Security Trust Fund account cannot be used as a piggy bank anymore to fund the current federal deficit. The Federal Reserve will need to find other ways to raise cash for the current operations of the federal government going forward. This is not necessarily a budgetary problem as long as the United States maintains a solid credit rating even during an economic crisis and lenders believe that it will someday pay its bonds when they become due. However, it is a concern because the federal government generates revenue from taxing workers, and the numbers of workers are declining and the tax system has not been modified to reduce the taxes paid by that smaller number of workers. Labor's share of the tax base is roughly 82 percent and trending higher, whereas the number of laborers is declining in relative numbers. This figure cannot be calculated exactly based on the business income data released by the IRS but suffice to say labor's share of the tax base is high and rapidly increasing.

ACCOUNTING FOR FEDERAL TAX REMITTANCES

To build on that explanation of the federal budget, and coherently discuss matters of accounting for tax remittances, the following sections cover some basic accounting questions and answers related to accounting for the federal budget.

The United States typically runs a budget deficit. How can you say workers fund transfer payments, or welfare, when the country is spending more than it takes in?

Answer: A budget deficit refers to negative income for the government during the year and reflecting at times an amount to be paid by future taxpayers. Despite reports that the national debt translates into some vast amount owed by each person or household in the United States, this is not entirely true: the government has both an income statement and a balance sheet with a variety of both assets *and* liabilities. Although this national balance sheet appears to be completely lost on politicians, the assets reflected on it mean that the deficit may not necessarily need to be paid off with future taxes.

An initial question of accounting, then, is who are the future taxpayers who might be required to pay taxes reflecting taxes not paid today? Taxpayers are mainly workers. The baseline assumption ought to be, then, that future taxpayers will be future workers, and accordingly, future workers will pay in more to offset the accumulated deficit. The accounting gimmick reflected in much of tax policy is to pretend that the future taxpayers will be wealthy persons as opposed to workers. The method used then also pretends that the deficit amount today should be attributable to future payments by the wealthy, so taxes should be reduced on the wealthy today. That approach is a deception or more aptly an accounting gimmick because baseline assumptions about future tax policy should or must reflect present reality. If assumptions about the present reality are to be changed in some way, then such changes must be clearly disclosed. In the absence of disclosure of assumptions, no person could know what the changes might be for the ultimate result, and the analysis could be misleading or ideological. Therefore, the starting point for any accounting method must always in some way relate to the present reality.

In the tax and social welfare system of the present day, the reality is that working people pay the bulk of the taxes. If workers pay the taxes today, then the starting point for any description of the future tax system must begin with the presumption that the workers will also pay the taxes tomorrow. That baseline assumption can be changed to some other imaginary state of affairs, but only if the change is expressly disclosed; for example,

> The methodology applied here presumes that the tax system will someday be changed so that the wealthy pay taxes disproportionately into the system and these payments are then used to fund transfer payments through the social benefit system. That assumption is reasonable for the following reasons.

Yet none of that explanation has been provided in research about tax remittances by the wealthy. The analysis is therefore incoherent because it has an inconsistent method of accounting for taxes remitted to the federal government. The approach has simply changed baseline assumptions about tax remittances without adequate disclosure—or any disclosure at all. Hence, the methodology of accounting for tax remittances is meant to deceive taxpayers who are not able to carefully study every detail. People who do not have time to look through every detail of the methodology are likely to presume that the methodology reflects the state of affairs under the present-day tax accounting methodology consistently applied forward into the future. But it absolutely does not! The methodology was switched to deceive the general public about the nature of tax remittances today and going forward into the future.

What does the term "income" mean in accounting?

Answer: Accounting methods are the means to understand both an economic concept of "income" (often thought of in economic terms as an accretion to wealth) versus cash flows. Hence, the accounting term "income" does not refer to cash flows. For example, a business that engages in shipbuilding may receive a contract to build a ship in Year 1, then build the ship over Years 2 and 3, and get paid for the ship upon completion and delivery to the buyer in Year 4. So, how should the shipbuilding company report "income" or profit on the sale? Should "income" be reported entirely in Year 1, incrementally in each of the Years 2 and 3 as the ship is constructed or only in Year 4? All of these are options for an accounting method. Each method would be better or worse depending on the purpose of the accounting process. All the various accounting methods available essentially allow current-year financial results to be understood in a different way not based just on cash flows. The different ways to account for "income" are thought to be helpful to the users of financial statements, such as investors, which is why businesses go through the trouble of preparing financial statements that report business income in different ways. Importantly, the differences in methods of accounting for "income" is not present with respect to most individual workers who are paid wages, so the "income" they receive generally matches their cash flow.

To apply the concept of income to the federal budget, when the Social Security Trust Fund ran a surplus, cash flow was positive, but that does not mean that the government had "income." The federal budget as a whole ran a surplus with positive "income" only recently, during the Clinton administration. A "deficit" means that the government ran a loss for the year, with negative income for the period. At nearly all other times in the history of the United States, the federal government was in a deficit (or loss) position in terms of "income" but was cash-flow positive because it was over-collecting taxes from workers. As the Baby Boomer generation continues to retire in the near future, the federal budget will then be in a deficit position *and* also turn cash-flow negative, as more benefits are paid out of the Social Security system than are collected from present workers.

What is a balance sheet versus an income statement, and why is this relevant to tax policy?

Answer: The federal budget is published on an annual basis (for the current year). However, many items of account in the budget span multiple years. So, there is a potential problem in saying how much of those items that span multiple years should be included in the current year. The field of accounting provides a means to solve that problem in a consistent way. However, the solutions are arbitrary because there are many ways to say what income or other balances are in a given period. Yet even though methods of accounting are arbitrary, by presenting the statements in a consistent way, results can be compared over multiple periods.

Thus, as a matter of accounting there are two statements of account: the income statement and the balance sheet. The income statement reflects events of the current year, and the balance sheet holds items that span multiple years. To fund the federal budget in terms of cash flow, the government historically moved items on and off the federal balance sheet, essentially a transfer from one statement to the other. At its most basic, this involves transferring an amount related to a past or future period into the current year.

The federal balance sheet is relevant to tax policy because the federal budget is funded partly by past and future tax payments. Many ideological claims of tax policy are premised on very unreasonable claims about the prospects for future tax payments and the identity of future taxpayers. Pertinent questions of tax policy are who are the future taxpayers likely to be and how much in taxes can they be expected to pay?

The Social Security Trust Fund no longer has a surplus, and funds might be taken from the general budget to fund welfare payments at some point in the future. So, income tax payments by the wealthy should account for some portions of future welfare payments right?

Answer: Not really. It is true that money is fungible, so one dollar here can be said to substitute for another dollar somewhere else. However, taxes levied on the wealthy and large corporations are declining as a share of the tax base. That means that the government will need to borrow relatively more to fund items on the income statement, and possibly to offset payable items on the balance sheet that turn out to be larger than estimated. Notably, it does not appear that large corporations will be asked to pay in relatively more, no matter how large the federal budget deficit might become. So, income taxes would not be attributable to transfer payments made out of the Social Security system in future periods either, at least by any methodology consistently applied in prior decades. To say that the wealthy pay monies that fund transfer payments, rather than only workers, the method of accounting needs to be changed to some other method *not* based on cash flows. Essentially, to posit the wealthy as the predominate taxpayer and source of the tax base, one needs to begin by creating a noncash-based method of accounting for tax remittances of some sort.

Is it possible for a worker to pay into the system and then draw out more benefits in cash than they have paid in?

Answer: Of course, it is possible for a worker to become disabled or sick and to draw out more than he or she paid into the system, but that difference is still paid for by other workers and not the wealthy or large corporations. With respect to individual workers within the Social Security system, running a quick mathematical spreadsheet of credits in versus debits out reveals that nearly all workers pay in more in cash than they get out (at least when all federal and state taxes are considered). Various Internet sources that say otherwise reflect accounting gimmicks to simply not count taxes paid by the working poor as a tax remittance. Notably, even an undocumented immigrant using a fake Social Security Number would still automatically pay Social Security taxes on wage earnings via withholding on any labor income and a host of other tax types, such as property tax, sales tax and gasoline tax, that would typically exceed any financial benefit from future transfer payments.

But lots of people with disabilities qualify for Social Security disability payments. Does that mean that they pay in more than they get out of the system without working?

Answer: No. Obviously, a person who never works could draw out more from a social benefit system than he or she pays in. Also, a person who works for a while but then becomes unable to work could draw out more than he or she pays in. Likewise, a person could live for a very long time and draw out more than he or she pays in. Yet, collectively workers pay in more on average than they get out of the system. And, in most cases, the taxes paid in for an individual worker exceed any benefits that might be received because there are so many other taxes paid at the state and local level. Even where the federal government pays out a net benefit to a disabled person, for example, much of that transfer payment is recaptured by other taxes levied on consumption by the federal or state and local governments, such as gasoline taxes or sales taxes.

Does it matter for tax policy that wealthier people tend to live longer than poorer people?

Answer: Yes. Because the wealthy live longer than the working poor, and studies have shown that the wealthy draw a disproportionate amount of benefits from the Social Security and Medicare systems. Federal transfer payments are also not means tested, so the wealthy receive a significant portion of transfer payments without any financial need for the benefits. In addition, the wealthy derive disproportionate benefits from various types of federal spending, such as in airports and the court systems, military spending and so on. Few low-income persons are engaged in international travel through airports, for example, and so do not gain much benefit from the massive federal expenditures on airports and airport security. Large corporations also derive revenue from the government directly, where the government purchases goods or services from the company. Yet, little or no prior scholarship attempts to measure the benefits received by the wealthy and large corporations for the value of directly and indirectly rendered government services.

Why is there so much misinformation on tax policy and social benefits?

Answer: A primary point of confusion appears to be the design of the Social Security system itself, which pays benefits to both retirees (especially long-lived retirees) and disabled persons.[4] This encourages people to think of Social Security beneficiaries as including past workers and disabled persons together. So, workers are associated with disabled persons and retirees within the Social Security system. However, that does not reflect what is really going on. In actual numbers, the beneficiaries should be considered as much wealthy persons who have long lifespans and people receiving Social Security disability as the working poor. The idea that the working class is drawing out a disproportionate amount of benefits from the social benefit system is simply incorrect. Rather, the working poor fund the Social Security system. The working poor generally die younger and do not live long enough to draw out substantially more than they paid in. Accordingly, when we speak of a "fiscal crisis of the welfare state," any crisis relates to a relatively smaller proportion of workers relative to retirees to pay wage taxes while the corporate share of the overall tax base is dramatically reduced. The origin of the "crisis" is more aptly thought of as the radical reductions in corporate taxation in the last several decades and culminating with the Tax Cuts and Jobs Act of 2017.

PUBLIC HEALTH AND WAGE TAXATION

Economists generally presume that all social science should begin with economics and are surprised to discover that's not the case. Economists even think that if something contrary to established economic doctrine is proposed, that contrary proposal must be wrong. This isn't true. Academic inquiry has indeed shifted away from the colonization by economics of other academic disciplines to the outright rejection of economics in other fields of social science as merely a type of disguised moral philosophy not in the nature of science or scientific inquiry.[5] Usually when an idea contrary to established doctrine becomes widely known, that new discovery turns out to contain at least some element of truth that makes is worthwhile and exciting to other scholars.

A few years ago, I published an article in the law journal *Wage Taxation and Public Health*.[6] The idea was simply that high rates of wage taxation should be considered harmful to the health outcomes of workers who are required to pay those taxes. The article was widely circulated and cited by other scholars in a range of scientific disciplines. I presented four theses in defense of this hypothesis on the relation between wage taxes and worker health. Three of those are as follows (for the fourth, see the next section):

1. Wage taxes push some workers into absolute poverty by payment of the tax.
2. Wage taxes may increase working hours for low-wage workers.
3. Wage taxes may increase inequality by levying higher rates of tax on persons with labor income.

The first thesis is straightforward: absolute poverty is known to be strongly associated with negative health outcomes. If wage taxes are levied at high rates and push some workers into absolute poverty, then it is reasonable to assume that these workers in absolute poverty experience negative health outcomes because of the tax levy.

The second thesis suggests that some workers may choose to work more hours in order to pay high rates of wage taxation. The increased workload is posited to be harmful to worker health. This thesis is consistent with prior research that links negative health outcomes to workload.

The third thesis is less intuitive, as it relies on a different line of social science research that suggests that relative economic inequality, as opposed to absolute poverty, is associated with negative health outcomes. Although it is not fully understood how or why relative economic inequality might cause negative health outcomes, the research nonetheless indicates that this is true.

Despite all this, the rather astonishing economic view on tax policy and public health is that taxes are good for public health. This is because it is presumed that redistributive taxation can be used to fund health initiatives that are good for public health. The premise is that taxes originate from the wealthy or large corporations and are redistributed for public health initiatives. William Savedoff explained as follows:

> Despite theoretical debates over the merits of consumption versus income taxes, national versus local, and earmarked versus general, the best guidance for tax policy is to focus on very pragmatic questions. Taxes should be raised keeping in mind the costs of tax administration, tax distortions in economy, and the politics of allocations (in the case of set-asides and earmarking). The net equity of health system financing depends more on the amount of funds that the tax system mobilizes and the way in which it is spent, than on the progressivity or regressivity of the taxes themselves.[7]

However, since the vast majority taxes are paid as withholding from paychecks of workers, the presumption that money might be used to alleviate public health concerns and that potential benefit might always exceed the social costs of high rates of wage taxation is neither justified nor plausible.

A significant problem with this view is that it purports to be a pragmatic approach to tax policy, but it is not, given its obvious flaw in identifying the source of tax levies. A pragmatic approach to tax policy might entail the application of a cash-based method of accounting for tax remittances, which economists rarely or never use in any context, including public health. Given the lack of cash-based methods of policy formation, it may be impossible for economic theory to be applied to a pragmatic approach in tax policy. The pragmatic view of tax policy must be to the contrary, that high rates of wage taxation levied on lower-income workers are likely to cause negative, not positive, health outcomes.

A further question is whether redistributive taxation could improve worker health outcomes; for example, the levying of taxes on lower-income workers with proceeds earmarked for health initiatives targeted to those very same lower-income workers and their families. This type of earmarking would have the effect of forcing the wage taxes to be spent on public health targeted to workers. Such an approach might be considered helpful where lower-income workers were thought to be underinvesting in their own health. The tax system would then essentially force workers into investing in their health. Notably, the investment in public health could have a greater positive benefit to workers than the negative or detrimental effect to worker health arising from payment of the tax. The obvious response to this argument is that there is no earmarking of wage taxes. Wage taxes are generally not spent on public health initiatives for workers who remit the tax. The tax system simply does not work that way. Rather, wage taxes are collected from workers and sometimes spent on health initiatives that target nonworking persons both rich and poor. Therefore, it is not possible to offset the detrimental health effects to lower-income workers from wage taxation with the health benefits from increased health spending under current tax laws.

INVESTMENT IN CHILDREN AND WAGE TAXATION

Workers are largely responsible for the health, safety and education of children. Insofar as the tax system takes money from workers via wage taxation, it indirectly allocates money away from children. Of course, this might be good or bad for society depending on whether and to what degree parental investment in children is thought to be desirable in economic terms; and whether sufficient investment is channeled to children by other means, such as public educational systems operated by local government. Worker capital is instead levied as tax and paid to the state without any subtraction for lost social benefits of how the money might otherwise have been spent, including as an investment in children. If there is an efficiency subtraction for alternate uses of worker capital in society, such as a disinvestment in children by wage taxation levied on their parents, then it is mostly missing from economic theory and tax policy. In point of fact, the design of tax policy hinges at least in part on whether investment in children by parents is considered desirable in economic terms.

The Internal Revenue Code contains provisions designed to offer financial incentives to families, such as the Child Tax Credit and the more favorable tax rates for persons with a "married" filing status. Previously, personal exemptions were provided for family members of the tax filer, but those were eliminated with the Tax Cuts and Jobs Act of 2017 in favor of larger standard deductions. These family-focused provisions seem to enjoy some political support in both parties. However, in recent decades, a host of scholars bitterly complained about the tax incentives for families largely on the grounds that this institutionalized a certain view of family. Irrespective of whether it is true that tax incentives to families implicitly marginalize other persons required to file a tax return, this concern reflects solely a moral or fairness argument. Very little of the extensive literature in law journals premised on this point of fairness has addressed whether family provisions were efficient or generated a return on investment from the furtherance of families, especially an incremental return on investment for low-income workers with otherwise limited means for investment in children.

The primary focus of this book is not to compare fairness ideas about the taxation of workers (and the families of workers) premised on various moral standards; instead it focuses on whether it is economically efficient to tax workers at high rates. This analysis of the economic effects to workers of high rates of wage taxation is relevant irrespective of the many justifications of moral philosophy as to why worker taxes or tax incentives for families might be considered fair or unfair. Accordingly, the question of whether financial incentives should be offered to working families could be analyzed not only on the grounds of fairness premised on moral philosophy but also as to whether an investment in children is efficient for society—or stated differently, whether investment in children generates an economic return greater than other possible investments.

The economic returns from public education are a good proxy to begin to estimate possible economic returns from parental investment in children. The returns to society of investing in public education appear to be impossibly high. Every human society that funds public education on a large scale seems to have outperformed every human society that failed to do so. Nonetheless, it is possible that there are declining returns to scale from education. That is, the returns from public education might be achieved at a relatively low level, then further investment in education might not generate an additional or incremental economic return. That is surely true at some level of investment, but in the United States we do not appear to have reached the point where educational investment begins to yield a declining return due to scale. To this day, roughly 40 percent of children in the United States live at or below the poverty line. The general lesson from public education is simply that any incremental investment in children appears to generate an astronomical return on investment. Although any declining returns of scale to child investment are currently unknown, American society is very far from any level of diminished returns if in fact there are declining returns to scale on child investment. Thus, any investment by parents in their own children should be expected to generate similar returns to the typical astronomical returns on investment of public education.

The high presumptive rates of return on public education strongly suggest that childhood education is a good economic investment for society. Modern social science has proved this indication beyond any possible doubt as public education is associated with better outcomes for children in nearly every possible positive-outcome and negative-outcome categories of measurement. Nonetheless, economic theory suggests the contrary: that the tax base should be shifted to workers to the extent possible even if this would reduce parental investment in children that is likely to generate spectacularly high economic returns to society. There is no empirical analysis whatsoever of the efficiency loss resulting from the use of high rates of worker taxation to take investment capital out of worker's hands. Local governments may then need to make incremental educational investments in children at very high cost because lower-income working parents lack the resources to do so: most of their surplus earnings are paid over to federal, state and local governments as wage taxes. This creates a very difficult political situation for a well-meaning person in local government. It is obvious that economic investment should be channeled into the children of the working poor to the extent possible at the local level, but those children will often leave the community as adults, so the community that makes the economic investment in its children will not enjoy the return on investment. This reflects a variation of the economic idea of the tragedy of the commons. The federal government exacerbates the problem by levying tax on workers at high rates at the national level.

An interesting question is why anyone might think that taxing workers does not create at least some efficiency loss due to disinvestment effects to children. The standard explanation appears to be as given by Malthus: the poor are presumed not to reinvest the proceeds of work in an efficient way. In Malthusian theory, workers do not deploy available capital into their own children. However, with the benefit of hindsight and better theory, we know this claim is false. Economic theory that proceeds on that Malthusian premise is also false; furthermore, economic theory that does not subtract efficiency losses due to high rates of wage taxation is severely flawed.

OBESITY AND WAGE TAXATION

A remarkable correlation exists in the public health and tax data gathered over the past several decades in the United States as follows: As the tax base has been assigned more and more to labor income as economists nearly unanimously recommend, workers have gotten more and more obese.[8] The trade-off appears to be roughly proportionate. As workers take on a greater portion of the tax base, they appear to get more obese at a constant rate. The rate of change between the variables can even be charted on roughly a straight line. In analytical terms, at the very least, the variables appear to have a strong correlation. As with any possible link between variables, the data depends on the statistical assumptions, yet the correlation appears to be undeniable. Therefore, the question should be asked, is this correlation merely a coincidence, or is it potentially causal, where relatively higher taxes on workers somehow cause an increase in obesity rates? In other words, as the relative taxes on workers are increased, is it true that workers become relatively more obese? One might even ask: Does economics have a consensus view as to why obesity has increased in the past several decades? The answer is no. The leading economic theorists have called for the identification of possible economic factors that might explain the trend of increases in obesity rates. Since economic theory focuses mostly on marginal tax rates, if effective tax rates were relevant to obesity, then this would be difficult for economists to find in any analysis of public health and tax policy.[9]

Does economics recognize that taxes on workers have increased over the past decades?

Answer: Remarkably, no. Economists counsel for assigning as much of the tax base to workers as possible by reducing the taxes on the wealthy and large corporations. However, at the same time, economists focus on the policy effects of marginal tax rates rather than effective tax rates. This has the practical effect of eliminating changes in the respective composition of the tax base from policy analysis. Therefore, as economists advise policymakers on matters of tax policy, there would not be any recognition that the share of the tax base assigned to labor has dramatically increased over time.

Is it possible that low wages, and not wage taxes, might cause increases in obesity?

Answer: Yes, absolutely. Mexico is usually reported to be the nation with the highest rates of obesity in the world and wages are very low. But low wages and high wage taxes may be two sides to the same coin. If wages are set to the minimum amount that workers can be expected to be paid to survive, then the relevant metric for public health analysis is the wage itself. However, if wages are set just above the survival level but then taxes are levied on the wages, the end result may be that the after-tax wage approximates the subsistence wage in the first instance. The economic effect to workers would be similar in both instances. Many of the economic effects of low wages in comparison to high taxes on wages might not be distinguishable between nations with different wage levels and tax systems.

Even if the tax base has shifted toward workers, if the taxes actually paid by workers have not increased, then how could this have a public health effect?

Answer: The gross amount of tax paid by individual workers is largely unknown, since the IRS does not release individual taxpayer data and reports data largely in the aggregate. The average tax assessment of lower-income workers does not appear to have markedly decreased due to changes in the statutory tax rate. Audit rates of persons claiming the earned income tax credit dramatically increased pursuant to a congressional mandate. This would indicate that taxes on those workers might have increased if the returns were adjusted. The IRS has also begun to computerize the system and issue electronic notices of assessment, often for very small amounts of tax, where an item reported on the tax return does not match electronic records. The issuance of these automated notices on a wide scale to lower-income workers could have the effect of increasing effective taxes on those workers. Any relative economic inequality has been shown to have impacts on health, so simply by reducing the tax rates on high earners while holding the taxes on lower-income workers constant could also yield a negative health effect.

Perhaps the most plausible explanation for how high taxes might have a public health effect is that the effective tax rates of workers and small businesses seem to have increased (or at least held constant) over a long period. A constant levy of high taxes on labor might be the causal factor, such that the health effects of high taxes on workers and small business may arise over a longer period. For example, a person might learn detrimental health behaviors early on influenced by the high rates of tax, and negative health effects would manifest only years later. An example would be lack of exercise or lack a healthy diet by a younger worker, who perhaps cannot afford to buy healthy food, and these behaviors might take ten to twenty years to reach full obesity recorded in medical records that could become known from economic surveys.

Why don't we have better data on the public health effects of changes in tax policy? Doesn't the lack of any economic analysis of the issue suggest that wages taxes must not have any health effect?

Answer: Not at all. Economics is the academic field broadly responsible for gathering data on taxes and tax policy. In most universities, only economists would have grants and support for empirical research on these topics. Economists thus have essentially a monopoly on empirical research in taxation. Economic journals often refuse to publish the findings if the analysis did not comport with the given economic ideology. Accordingly, if economic theory does not broach topics relevant to tax policy, then it is possible that the relevant empirical evidence would simply not be gathered at all because it does not fit the accepted theory. The first step in empirical analysis is accordingly to correct the underlying flaw in the theory. Empirical analysis can really begin only after the flaw is corrected. If a strong correlation exists between obesity and wage taxes, this at the very least merits further investigation and research by tax scholars. The lack of any prior empirical economic research on matters not fitted to economic theory does not yield any indication about the veracity of those ideas.

SMALL BUSINESS AND WAGE TAXATION

One difference between economic theory (as applied to tax policy) and business theory as taught in business schools might be called the origins of capital for investment. In one iteration of Harberger's small open-economy model, the aggregate capital stock is taken as a fixed amount worldwide. Under this view, tax policy should be designed so as to draw in some of the capital stock into the domestic economy. If economic activity requires both capital and labor, then the absence of capital in the economy would prevent or decrease economic activity. Under that view, no modeling is really required to conclude that the tax system should be designed as favorable to capital. If the tax system is not set up to be favorable to capital, then capital won't be drawn into the jurisdiction, as a hummingbird may be drawn to a flower. We could really call Harberger's model the "hummingbird and flower" model of tax incidence rather than the small open-economy model. Of course, the process of corporate tax competition, designed to set corporate tax rates as low as possible, is all premised on some version of the hummingbird model.

Yet the premise of economic theory that forms the basis for all modern tax policy is not at all how businesses, especially small businesses, operate in the economy. Small businesses usually proceed to build their own sources of capital from successful operation of the business. In many cases, the labor of the small business owner is the source of capital. The idea is that capital is self-created and thus not necessarily drawn in through investors from overseas. Small businesses often reinvest capital from prior profits, or even borrow from the bank, to make a business investment. Thus, the increase in capital to fund economic expansion would arise on lower taxes on the group of people likely to engage in business reinvestment, namely small business. As already explained, large corporations have been very reluctant to reinvest profits into the economy. The lack of reinvestment into capital assets is the general reason large corporations have been so insistent on reducing the statutory tax rate.

SOCIAL COSTS OF AUTOMATION AND ROBOT WORKERS

Perhaps the most incredible aspect of US tax policy are the multiple layers of corporate tax competition. Corporate tax competition refers to the idea that nations compete for capital investment by setting their tax rates as low as possible. To justify tax policy along these lines, economists urge that corporate tax rates be set as low as possible to encourage capital to flow into the jurisdiction. Economists then urge that domestic tax rates on capital again need to be reduced to encourage investment in automation, such as robot workers. The basic idea is that firms would choose to automate in lower-taxed jurisdictions, notwithstanding the contrary reality that nations with the highest degree of automation seem also to have some of the higher shares of taxes to GDP, such as Japan and Finland. To my knowledge, no economic study has set out to examine, even in theory, whether corporate tax competition from lower rates might impact other domestic versions of tax competition that set out to favor robots. This is an incredible methodology and an approach unique to economic policy, at least, as far as I can tell. For example, imagine the economic approach to tax policy applied in a medical context, such as if a doctor simultaneously prescribed two drugs, like aspirin and ibuprofen, and failed to evaluate whether the combination of those drugs might create unexpected or undesirable results to the patient. The economic prescription for corporate tax competition of a reduction in corporate tax rates and then the offering of additional special tax incentives for robots and automation to the corporations using those robots, is analogous to that illustration and would be considered abjectly ridiculous in other contexts.

The perceived benefit of automation seems to be that automation is thought to be efficient because robots can perform work at a lower cost than human beings. Maybe. Perhaps large firms choose to automate because of the tax benefits afforded to robot workers as opposed to human workers. But, an even better question is why automation seems to occur predominantly in higher-tax jurisdictions and almost never in tax havens. Large firms seem to choose to automate at least in part to avoid the high taxes levied on human workers. The extremely high taxes on workers make human labor more expensive relative to robot workers. Therefore, firms may choose to use robot workers even where human workers are more efficient than robots in order to avoid the taxes. There are various ways that robot workers are favored over human workers in the tax system, ranging from the differential in tax rates to the various types of wage tax levied exclusively on human workers and consumption taxes that only humans pay.[10]

The unanswered question relating to the effects of corporate tax competition is: What are the social costs of increased automation? Or, are there both benefits and *costs* to automation, or only benefits? It turns out there are costs, including social costs, to automation. Perhaps the most important of these is a reduction in gross tax revenue when a robot worker replaces a human worker. Since human workers are taxed a lot and capital is not taxed very much, and since robots are a type of capital investment, if a robot replaces a human, each time this occurs the government goes from collecting an amount equal to perhaps 50 percent or more of the gross wages paid to the human to instead collecting an amount likely close to $0 in tax from the corporation that operates the robot. Furthermore, there is no guarantee that efficiency has increased due to the automation either, since the firm may have chosen to automate solely to obtain the tax benefit, not for reasons of economic efficiency. If so, economic activity would not expand as a result of the automation. The only economic effect from automation could be a decrease in tax collections without any efficiency gains.

If that weren't bad enough, many scholars have posited significant social costs to the human workers replaced by the robots. This has led to various calls for a universal income guarantee in order to offset some of the social costs. For example, perhaps that human worker needs to be retrained in another field or may even become unemployed and begin to draw on the social benefit system as a result of automation. Therefore, it seems likely that tax revenue may decline precipitously at the very time that revenue is needed to retrain human workers potentially displaced by automation.

HOW PIKETTY VASTLY UNDERSTATED INEQUALITY IN THE UNITED STATES

Perhaps the most significant tax publication of the past decade was Thomas Piketty's book on economic inequality, *Capital in the Twenty-First Century*.[11] Piketty and his coauthor in the initial journal publication obtained special access to IRS data on tax returns filed by Americans over the past fifty years or so. The tax return data were then used to generate claims about changes in economic inequality. And that approach at least initially seems like a viable method to identify changes or trends in levels of economic inequality over time. If the wealthy were getting richer relative to the poor, then the first place you should expect that wealth to show up is on the tax return, right? Wrong.

Inequality is increasing in the United States. However, the predominant reason for the increase in inequality is the higher taxes paid by workers relative to the wealthy. As the wealthy continuously reinvest the proceeds of tax avoidance, the compound returns add up to a significant portion of the total economic output of the United States. I've previously calculated the shift in inequality between the wealthy and the poor due to the differential in effective tax rates to be roughly 2 percent of the total gross national product of the United States as taken over a 10-year period.[12] In other words, of all the wealth produced in the United States in a year, at least 2 percent of it is attributable exclusively to the lessor tax rate paid by the wealthy.

One premise of this chapter is that the wealthy do not pay much tax relative to their income or wealth even though the income tax rates are progressive. How can this be? The claim appears paradoxical because working people seem to always pay tax on income that is reported on their tax return. Don't the wealthy do the same? It should be possible to determine changes in inequality from the face of the tax return as Piketty purported to do, right? Nope.

In many years, the predominant form of "income" enjoyed by the wealthy is the appreciation on capital assets, referred to by the Federal Reserve as "holding gains."[13] This means accrual gains on capital assets, which have not necessarily been sold during the year and would include things like stock market gains, home value appreciation or other gains on real property. Nearly all of these capital assets are held by the wealthy. However, these amounts are not necessarily reported on any tax return. Holding gains tend to increase relative to other types of income during bull stock market years—and this is especially true over the past decade as the price of capital assets has rapidly increased. The amounts of holding gains are tracked by the Federal Reserve and have reached astronomical levels in the past few years. Thus, to determine inequality, one would need to add the amounts of holding gains to the income of the wealthy. Piketty did not do so in the measurement of inequality, so the amount of reported inequality is drastically understated.

EXPLANATION OF THE TERM: TAXABLE INCOME

A misunderstood aspect of inequality relates to what tax experts refer to as "taxable income." Taxable income is a legal and accounting concept that represents the amount of income reported on the tax return and subjected to tax. So, it represents only an amount of income after all tax avoidance planning, such as that of tax lawyer and accountants. The confusion seems to arise as for workers wages received are generally taxable income. However, the primary difference between taxable income and total income is holding gains as reported by the Federal Reserve. If the capital assets to which holding gains relate have not been sold, then these amounts are generally not included in taxable income.

PROGRESSIVE OR REGRESSIVE TAX SYSTEM

The news media often reports that statutory tax rates in the United States are progressive. This is true. If a person with predominantly labor income earns more, such as a nurse who picks up extra shifts at the hospital, this may result in the worker moving into a higher tax bracket and remitting more income tax. However, tax remittances are generally not calculated for wealthier people using solely the statutory tax rate. The progressivity of the rate structure is not really the primary concern of tax accountants and lawyers. Most of what tax accountants and lawyers do is tax planning designed to reduce the taxable base upon which a tax rate will be applied. As it happens, tax avoidance planning designed to reduce the taxable base works quite well for income derived from capital, and hardly at all for income derived from labor. Partly for this reason, it is necessary to discuss tax rates on an effective basis and not a statutory basis.

The regressivity of the US tax system arises mostly because of the special tax treatment of wage earnings. Wage earnings are taxed twice—once as wages and again as income. For example, if a person works and earns $50,000 in wages over the course of a year, that person first pays wage withholding taxes of 6.2 percent for Social Security plus 1.45 percent for Medicare (each of which the employer also matches). The worker never receives the withheld funds, in excess in this example of $3,200 (notably, that's just the federal portion, excluding state wage and income taxes typically applied in the same fashion). Next, the worker must file a federal income tax return reporting $50,000 in wage earnings including the portion withheld by the federal and state governments and then pay tax on those earnings again, amazingly, for earnings never actually received. Such double taxation of labor earnings is the most common instance of double taxation in the United States today. The second income taxation of wage withholdings never received was at one point challenged under the Sixteenth Amendment. The end result of the overall design of the tax system is a very high effective tax rate on workers who derive income from labor. A third explanation for the regressivity of the overall tax system is other forms of taxation (apart from federal income taxation), which are disproportionately paid by lower-income persons. These include federal wage, gasoline, excise, state income, state wage, sales, property (in the form of higher rent) and many fees in the nature of income taxes. Notably, in the seminal decision *NFIB v. Sebelius*, the Supreme Court held that penalties or fees are classifiable as "taxes."

On an overall effective rate basis, the tax system in the United States is sharply regressive. The following table shows that the effective tax rate is very low for the top earners, who pay roughly one-third the tax rate of other taxpayers.

EFFECTIVE TAX RATES OF INDIVIDUALS BY INCOME QUINTILE (2012)

US Persons	Bottom 20%	Second	Third	Fourth	Top 20%
Effective Tax Rate:	27%	25%	24%	23%	9%

Data Source : Bureau of Labor Statistics, Consumer Expenditure Survey (2012); Federal Reserve, Z1 Report (2012); Bret N. Bogenschneider, *The Effective Tax Rate of U.S. Persons by Income Level*, 145 TAX NOTES 117 (2014).

These figures reflect all taxes that each quintile is required to pay based on available government data. The estimates are conservative—the tax rates on the bottom income group are much higher (over 50 percent) if educational expenditures and health insurance costs are included. The net regressivity of the tax system is reflected in that each of the lower four quintiles pays roughly triple the effective tax rate of the highest-income quintile. This is true when all taxes are taken into account, including unrealized capital gains, or holding gains. The Federal Reserve publishes the amount of accrued but untaxed capital gains in its economic reports to render an effective rate calculation possible. Since the wealthy accrue the vast majority of holding gains, and also, most income not derived from holding gains, it is hardly surprising that the wealthy would also pay most of the income taxes. If income were more evenly distributed, federal income taxes would automatically become more evenly distributed. In any case, once all types of taxation are taken into account, the tax system is revealed as regressive, not progressive.

NOTES

1 Reuven Avi-Yonah, *Globalization, Tax Competition, and the Fiscal Crisis of the Welfare State*, 113 HARV. L. REV. 7 (2000).

2 See Nat'l Academies of Science, Eng'g & Med., *The Growing Gap in Life Expectancy by Income: Implications for Federal Programs and Policy Responses* (Washington, DC: National Academies Press, 2015).

3 See Organization for Economic Cooperation and Development, (http://www.oecd.org). Accessed Nov. 10, 2019.

4 See Frank Ramsey, *A Contribution to the Theory of Taxation*, 37 ECON. J. 47 (1927) ("The effect of taxation is to transfer income in the first place from individuals to the State and then, in part, back again to rentiers and pensioners.").

5 Donald N. McCloskey, *The Rhetoric of Economics,* 21 J. ECON. LIT. 481 (1983), at 513 ("Economics has [...] become imperialistic. There is now an economics of history, of sociology, of law, of anthropology, of politics, of political philosophy, of ethics.

The flabby methodology of modernist economics simply makes this colonization more difficult, raising irrelevant methodological doubts in the minds of the colonized folk.").

6 Bret N. Bogenschneider, *Wage Taxation and Public Health*, 14 RUTGERS J.L. & PUB. POL'Y 1 (2016).

7 World Health Organization, *Tax-Based Financing for Health Systems: Options and Experiences* (Discussion Paper No. 4, 2004).

8 Bret N. Bogenschneider, *Is the Design of the Tax System a Causal Factor for Obesity?* 3:22 QUINNIPIAC HEALTH L. R. 323 (2019).

9 Ibid.

10 For further analysis of the effect of the taxation of robots on tax policy, see Ryan Abbott & Bret N. Bogenschneider, *Should Robots Pay Taxes? Tax Policy in the Age of Automation*, 12 HARV. LAW & POL'Y REV. 145 (2017).

11 See Thomas Piketty & Immanuel Saez, *Income Inequality in the United States, 1913–1998**, 118 QUART. J. ECON. (2003).

12 Bret N. Bogenschneider, *Income Inequality & Regressive Taxation in the United States*, 4:3 INT. J. ECON. & BUS. LAW 8 (2015).

13 Federal Reserve economic data including holding gains is available at the website, https://www.federalreserve.gov/datadownload/Build.aspx?rel=Z1. Accessed Nov. 10, 2019.

CONCLUSION: POSTMODERN TAX POLICY, OR WHY THE "LITTLE PEOPLE" MATTER TO TAX POLICY

All of tax policy is designed toward one end: to assign as much of the tax base to workers as possible and thereby avoid the levy of tax on the wealthy and large corporations. The tax system allows the wealthy and large corporations to exercise power by avoiding tax.[1] As Leona Helmsley famously said, "We don't pay taxes. Only the 'little people' pay taxes."[2] Nearly every economic metric on taxation, including every tax statistic, tax law or regulation, and political statement on tax policy, comprises a subtle trick or outright deception and coercion toward this end. The various debates in tax policy circles leading up to the passage of the Tax Cuts and Jobs Act of 2017 with respect to "corporate inversions" and "corporate tax competition" reflect these types of deceptions and were intended to set the political stage for corporate tax cuts. The political ideology of tax policy reflects the distribution of power in modern society and has little or nothing to do with fostering efficiency or fairness. The prior applications of supposed postmodern thought in tax policy have been premised on group identity and missed the larger point that the tax system is designed to soak the workers. Most experts in taxation and tax policy, including especially tax practitioners who deal with taxes on a daily basis, are fully aware of this reality and simply accept it without further reflection and move on.

The more important point is that the tax system allows the rich to feel powerful in their pursuit of tax avoidance, which they most often achieve by tax avoidance planning as a means of overcoming the tax law otherwise applicable to the "little people." As the prime example of the pursuit of power through tax avoidance schemes, again take Leona Helmsley. Helmsley, for example, who avoided paying sales taxes on her jewelry by putting the necklace on in New York City and mailing an empty box from the jewelry store to her out-of-state residence in New Jersey, where New York sales tax did not apply. Helmsley and her statement on the "little people" provide a key insight—it is not the money savings from tax avoidance that is the important thing to many wealthy persons, but the feeling of overcoming the tax law in a way not available to the "little people."

The reference to the "little people" as the other group in society is a significant feature of the tax system. If it did not offer to the wealthy a means to avoid the tax system, then the wealthy would endeavor to change the system through the political process and the lobbying of elected representatives. The feeling of power to the wealthy is the key aspect of the whole endeavor of tax policy, not just the actual dollar savings. Simply put, the wealthy, such as Helmsley, are willing to pay some tax as long as the "little people" are required to pay even more. The acceptability of taxes to the ruling class may hinge on the requirement that the ruled classes are required to pay more. Furthermore, the "ruling class" in any society might be actually defined as the group that is not required to pay taxes—I think that definition would largely hold in historical terms. For example, in Greek democracy the benefit of the democratic process was largely seen as the repeal of regressive tax types.

If it is true that workers are simply the less powerful group, then it is they who are required to pay taxes in society. The requirement for workers to pay the taxes is indeed the default rule of tax policy today; accordingly, there is nothing about the design of the tax system that is directly related to fairness concerns identified from the perspective of workers. Since workers pay the bulk of the taxes as measured on a cash basis, the many volumes of moral philosophy on the topic of taxation written by Robert Nozick, John Rawls, Richard Epstein and so on, tell us very little about the respective fairness of tax policy; these philosophical writings can be understood instead as justifications of the current tax system written on behalf of the wealthy to help them feel better about not paying taxes or to feel superior in the overcoming of tax laws that otherwise apply against the "little people." In some cases, such as the writings of Epstein, the moral framework has hidden within it a special accounting method by which to count beans that favors the wealthy. By inconsistently applying that method of accounting for tax remittances to different groups of taxpayers, it is possible to use the moral framework to reach nearly any statistical or moral result. A prerequisite to moral philosophizing about tax policy can thus be understood as a commitment to consistently apply methods of accounting to reach moral results.

In comparison, when the wealthy or large corporations pay tax, economists wrongly think their doing so is inefficient and therefore wrong in moral terms.

Yet, I see almost nothing unique about the ways that the wealthy choose to allocate capital compared to members of the working class, that would justify setting tax policy using that rationale. If fairness rather than efficiency is the ultimate objective, then even philosophically liberal philosophical writings by John Rawls and others provide merely the preconditions that would be needed for redistribution through the tax system such that under those conditions the system would be considered "fair." Examples are progressivity in tax rates or taxes to be used for redistribution for basic needs of the needy. Such preconditions are largely presumed to be met in modern society through progressive federal income tax rates and by welfare or other social programs. The rate progressivity and welfare programs are thereby taken together to establish that the current taxation system is "fair" for society as a whole. But the tax system is more accurately described as designed to collect money from workers and redistribute that money to non-workers, rich and poor. Redistribution largely does not occur from the wealthy to the poor, but from the workers to the poor. We have not reached the true philosophical question whether it is "fair" for the tax system to tax the workers to fund the basic needs of the poor while the wealthy stand guard over accumulated hoards of un-taxed capital.

The elements of the postmodern view of tax policy described throughout this book can be summarized more specifically as follows:

1. Economics and the origins of tax policy. Economic theory in respect of taxation comprises mostly justification as opposed to policy analysis and is always designed to favor the interests of the wealthy and large corporations over the interests of workers. Furthermore, there is little or no empirical evidence for most economic claims on tax policy. The various models used in economics as a substitute for scientific methods generally do not relate to the actual world, and no attempt is made to check whether such models correspond to actual. Economic descriptions of tax policy do not reflect methods of modern scientific inquiry and are often derived from historical versions of science popular in the mid- to late seventeenth century. Economic theories and models relevant to tax policy, such as the Laffer curve, are almost never subject to test even when their predictions are observed to be false. The given epistemology of economics is essentially unworkable as applied to tax policy.

2. Limitations on the use of moral philosophy in formulating tax policy. Moral philosophy comprises standards to determine what counts as a consequence in determining the fairness of tax policy. However, moral philosophy as applied to tax lacks any accounting method or coherent means to count the consequences. This means the moral results are unknowable and often

misleading or even wrong. The standards of moral philosophy in taxation have been targeted almost exclusively at the wealthy as a means to justify an oppressive tax system. The negative effects of labor taxation to workers are rarely, if ever, counted as a consequence in any of the standard interpretations of liberal, economic or libertarian theory. A better interpretation of libertarianism is that the various effects of the heavy taxation of workers should count as a consequence in that particular moral framework.

3. The social costs of wage taxation. The purpose of the tax system is to collect nearly all tax revenue from workers and to help the wealthy justify the oppressive nature of the tax system. However, any tax system so designed to make the wealthy feel good is inherently inefficient. The overtaxation of small business reduces economic growth to near zero by eliminating the competition to large corporations in many domestic markets. The over-taxation of workers leads to negative public health effects to workers and their children, such as obesity. It is not at all clear that the tax revenue raised from the heavy taxation of workers exceeds the social costs created by the levy of these taxes.

4. The exclusion of the "little people" from tax policy. The "little people" will only begin to count if they insist on being counted as part of the democratic discourse on matters of tax policy. The deceptive tactics of tax scholars and other commentators have largely prevented the "little people" from expressing a voice in tax policy.

WHY CHANGING THE TAX LAWS WILL NOT SOLVE THE PROBLEM

The Internal Revenue Service (IRS) generally does not set out to enforce existing tax law against US corporations. It follows a "policy of restraint," meaning that it does not request FIN48 records on uncertain tax positions reflecting the aggressive tax planning of large corporations to defeat tax that are required to be prepared with the financial statements. The IRS *does* aggressively audit recipients of the earned income tax credit down to the last dollar. A new project referred to as cooperative compliance proposes to go even further down the road of nonenforcement of the existing tax laws against large corporations and their "well-educated" management teams who are essentially presumed to never engage in tax avoidance activity.[3]

Tax avoidance planning by tax lawyers and accountants is performed almost exclusively on behalf of the wealthy. Hence, tax practitioners know by practical experience that workers pay the taxes in society. Tax professionals profit partly by furthering the system and aiding the wealthy and large corporations in tax avoidance. It is simply not profitable for tax practitioners to talk about the hidden truths of taxation and tax policy as set forth in this book. The extraordinary complexity of tax rules also partly necessitates the business of accounting and lawyering with respect to taxation. The complexity also means that it is possible to avoid tax partly by careful tax planning but especially by hiring insiders with special knowledge about tax and paying them handsomely.

All legal practice in tax law depends on "legal indeterminacy." The indeterminacy of law represents the vagueness inherent in tax legislation, such as the Internal Revenue Code and the accompanying regulations. Tax laws are gray, not black and white. Lots of people who don't know much of anything about tax think that tax laws must be black-and-white; otherwise, such laws could be invalidated by courts. That is wrong: no tax law can be drafted to cover every possible future scenario. The wrong idea is that all tax laws should be known in advance irrespective of whether the taxpayer, especially when a large corporation, may have gone to great lengths to create special situations that do not fit the tax law exactly. The inherent challenge or difficulty in tax law is in drafting laws to cover every possible situation that may arise in the future. Most of what tax lawyers do is try to fit unexpected tax scenarios into various provisions of the Internal Revenue Code, a process known as "legal interpretation."

Tax lawyers engage in tax avoidance planning by creating special sets of facts that do not fit exactly in the law. This creates uncertainty in legal interpretation, or legal indeterminacy. The pertinent legal question is what to do with uncertainty arising in the tax laws from specially "manufactured" factual situations created by multinational firms (in collusion with accounting and law firms that spread ideas about how to create indeterminacy). The consensus conclusion in US law journals is that there can be no answer because the moral standards are inconclusive.[4] That is, so many tax articles have been written from so many different moral perspectives that there are good reasons to use Rawls or Locke as illustration, and this might yield different conclusions, so nothing can really be said about rightness or fairness. Notably, the legal focus on rightness has often been overborne by economic ideals of efficiency, so it also happens that judges or tax lawyers can find ways in legal decisions to avoid taxing multinational firms because they believe it to be inherently efficient and therefore right.[5]

The debate over taxation and tax theory in Anglo-American legal circles often centers on citations to various philosophers in an attempt to say that a given proposal is justified, including by reference John Rawls, John Locke and

Robert Nozick.[6] The legal approach is partly an attempt to influence the political process through democratic discourse (by Rortyan means), but it also reflects a presumption that laws, such as the Internal Revenue Code, are not valid in full. Broadly speaking, this means that there are factual situations that will arise that the law does not expressly cover; then a standard apart from the positive law (or, tax code) itself will be necessary to decide what to do in specific legal contexts, such as moral frameworks. In Continental Europe, laws are often taken to be fully valid, meaning the code itself should provide the answer to questions, often by an implicit method of legal interpretation drawn out from within the statute. Accountants in the United States often follow a similar approach, as for the vast majority of situations the answer to tax questions is clear on the face of the law. However, the practice of multinational firms is to take advantage of the possibility of indeterminacy and to *manufacture* indeterminacy, which means to intentionally create factual situations that are not expressly covered by the tax law in order to avoid tax.[7] Hence, the novel factual situations that comprise the common law of taxation only exist because multinational firms have gone to great lengths to intentionally create indeterminacy within the tax laws.

By this stylized legal approach, only large multinational firms and very wealthy individuals are able to engage in the creation of indeterminate factual situations to trigger legal review. All wage-earning persons must simply pay tax, and they have no legal rights in respect of taxation. In the rare situation that an individual person makes a viable challenge to a tax law, such as by challenging the double taxation of wage earnings, that taxpayer is subject to penalties or sanctions.[8] The entire system of tax law has marginalized and eliminated the individual and small-business taxpayer. In philosophical terms, this means that the "little people" are covered by a different set of rigid laws than the wealthy, and also forced to remit an ever-increasing portion of the tax base. Meaningful tax reform does not begin by changing the statutory tax rates. The statutory tax rates are designed to and do generally apply against the "little people" with predominantly wage income, which is not eligible to be deferred or reduced by netting with deductions. Any increase in a progressive statutory tax rate might even have a regressive effect. The first step in meaningful tax reform is rather to take away the power of the wealthy to avoid tax within the tax system.

POSTMODERN TAX POLICY

The philosopher Richard Rorty challenged the given epistemology of science. A challenge to epistemology reflects a postmodern approach. As applied to taxation, a postmodern critique means that the various ways that economists, politicians and philosophers say they "know" things about taxation are not objective, but reflect the biases and beliefs of those persons. Rorty made the important postmodern point that the criteria that persons choose to know things simply reflect back on the person doing the choosing like a mirror. Since after such a successful postmodern critique there is nothing left that is objective, all that is left after postmodernism is discourse among persons in a democracy, here, democratic discourse over tax policy. Accordingly, an appropriate response to a person who claims to know things about taxation and tax policy is to reference the democratic debates over that topic.

Recent polling evidence suggests a majority of US persons opposed the Tax Cuts and Jobs Act of 2017,[9] which reduced the corporate tax rate from 35 percent to 21 percent and granted other benefits especially to large multinational firms. This polling data is potentially significant because it suggests that tax policy has not deceived everyone. Some Americans realize that the political discourse on tax policy is a deception. Other Americans might not know exactly how they were tricked on taxes, but they know they were tricked. The democratic populace has thus listened to predictions of "trickle-down" economic growth for decades, as this idea hasn't shown results workers have become increasingly cynical and frustrated with tax policy.

If Rorty was correct at all that epistemology is subject to critique by reference to democratic discourse, then surely the lack of enthusiasm over the cornerstone trickle-down ideas of tax policy in economic theory is significant.[10] The field of critical tax studies has not adopted this aspect of postmodern philosophy because the prior assumption has always been that democratic opinion manifested in the system of tax laws must be designed to oppress various groups known by identity. However, in light of the Tax Cuts and Jobs Act of 2017, the tax system does not appear to always reflect popular opinion in the democracy. The lack of political support for the Tax Cuts and Jobs Act of 2017 reflects the cynicism of most Americans, who are well aware that the discussion of tax policy is based on deception. The view of the working classes appears to often arise from the application of a cash-based method of accounting to tax policy which is not an unreasonable choice in strictly accounting terms.

Political discourse on tax policy typically involves discussions of what to do with the proceeds of wage taxes on workers and how to redistribute money from workers to others. Sometimes political discourse extends to discussions of how to generously reallocate back to workers some of the monies taken from them by wage taxes. The primary function of moral philosophy is to justify a system where workers are picked clean of any residual profit from work. By applications of moral philosophy to justify the heavy taxation of workers, wealthy persons are able to justify the continued pursuit of the accumulation of huge fortunes and the diversion of monies into palaces and yachts. Yet contrary to some teachings of economics, yacht-building is not necessarily efficient for society even if it creates jobs. Some types of assets create an economic return and some do not. Yachts and palaces do not create an economic return absent the positing of categories within international taxation; that is, one might say that an industry of domestic yacht-building is beneficial to the host country. In any case, there are qualitative differences in the projects to which workers are deployed. Wealthy people have been making themselves comfortable by building pleasure palaces for thousands of years. Yet work intended to make the wealthy comfortable does not automatically yield an efficiency gain unless domestic workers were building yachts for overseas billionaires, and so on. The idea that it is good for society to use tax avoidance to accumulate funds to build palaces to make the wealthy comfortable is not a new idea, and the economic writings that describe this type of capital investment as "efficient" for various reasons are categorically mistaken.

WHY THE "LITTLE PEOPLE" MATTER TO TAX POLICY

The federal budget is composed almost entirely of proceeds from the taxation of work (and current borrowing therefrom out of the savings of workers in the Social Security system) as derived by wage taxation. Wages are taxed in a multiplicity of different ways. Much of the television commentary to the contrary reflects accounting gimmicks premised on not counting the taxes paid by workers. These deceptions are just a trick, no more intellectually significant than a tavern card player pulling an ace from up his sleeve and dropping it on the table. An Internet search on tax policy reflects what is essentially a card trick with the widespread claims that the wealthy pay more than 50 percent of the income taxes and the "little people" pay 1 percent of the income taxes. But, it is sheer nonsense to suggest that workers in the United States do not pay much in taxes, and by "nonsense" I mean to say the creation of an entirely new system of accounting to generate the nonsensical result. Amazingly, this stylized accounting chant of tax remittances is repeated even where the Social Security Trust Fund has been raided over the years to fund the federal government. This claim is so misleading it essentially proves that there is nothing coherent in the discussion of tax policy. Tax policy rather compiles justifications of a tax system where workers pay as much of the tax base as they are able to bear at any point in time.

Economic theory posits a "deadweight loss" from progressive income taxation, solely on the wealthy, where high-income persons supposedly cut back on economic output due to high rates of taxation.[11] The study used to justify this idea back in the 1990s was flawed and invalid.[12] However, the basic line of thought on taxation remains within economic theory: in efficiency terms when the poorer workers pay taxes, this is good, when the rich pay taxes, this is bad. Therefore, when economists set out to measure tax policy, they apply a subtraction from economic growth referred to as the deadweight loss. However, there is *not* a corresponding loss from economic growth when the poor pay taxes.[13] This approach reflects one of the underlying premises of "trickle-down" economic thought on the subject of tax policy.

The meaning of the term "tax cuts" has further changed from debates on tax reform during the Reagan administration. The term "tax cuts" now refers to the federal government setting out to borrow additional money through the tax system and to indirectly transfer it to large corporations as a form of stimulus. This indirect transfer is achieved partly by reducing the corporate tax rate, as occurred with the Tax Cuts and Jobs Act of 2017, but also by allowing large corporations to aggressively take advantage of the indeterminacy of tax laws and the lack of enforcement of existing tax laws against large corporations, especially with respect to transfer pricing. If history is any guide, stimulus in the form of tax breaks for the wealthy and large corporations will result in another dramatic boom-and-recession cycle. Except this time things have changed. The Social Security Trust Fund is nearly exhausted. Worker savings cannot be used to fund any further corporate tax cuts. Therefore, the next time funds are needed, wage taxes will have to be *increased*. All prior economic events have been designed to transfer the Social Security Trust Fund to large corporations through the tax system, and future economic events will be designed to collect additional tax revenue from current and future generations of workers. That is the postmodern view on taxes and tax policy.

Nearly all the evidence suggests that when the poor pay taxes, it is harmful to society.[14] A truly amusing recent article was titled "Why aren't most Americans rich? These theories might help explain it."[15] The article describes several character flaws of the poor in America, who supposedly lack the ability to budget and save. Such articles make the wealthy feel good about having superior character. Yet the obvious reason more Americans are not rich is the high taxes levied on labor income in comparison to capital income. Only those persons who are able to hold capital can avoid the very high tax rates that allow wealth accumulation to occur. Persons who simply work end up paying so much tax that it is extremely difficult for them to accumulate much capital at all.

The truth is that workers are required to pay the bulk of taxes in human society—this is the foremost rule of economic theory as applied to tax policy. Thomas Malthus, widely regarded as the world's first economist, justified that core belief when he explained the poor would simply waste away the proceeds of work in the alehouse. Economics has not strayed very far from its origins in Malthusian thought in the interceding centuries. However, economics differs from tax practice in that economists have almost no practical knowledge of the tax system or how it works but deeply believe that it is somehow efficient for workers to pay taxes. The truth is that the tax system is not fair at all or efficient, nor is it intended to be fair or efficient.

Let us start over in tax policy with the very reasonable presumption that taxes are harmful to all persons, not just the wealthy, including the working poor and their children. If the poor are harmed by taxation it is unreasonable to suggest that only when the rich spend money is it "efficient" for the economy; it should also be possible that similar or even greater efficiency gains could be achieved by reducing taxes on workers and allowing them to spend that money in the furtherance of small business activity. Also, where workers and the working poor are forced into difficult economic decisions by low wages and regressive taxation, especially as related to food choice and health, this is harmful to society. Thus, if there is any possibility that levying high effective tax rates on the working poor might harm them or force them into "bad" choices, then these social costs constitute a subtraction from economic results. The existence of that efficiency subtraction from taxes levied on workers is beyond any reasonable dispute as a matter of science, yet it is conspicuously absent from the current economic theory of tax policy. Finally, it should be plainly obvious based on the data that rapid economic growth could be encouraged via tax policy by reducing the overwhelming taxes on small business activity.

NOTES

1 Bret N. Bogenschneider, *The Will to Tax Avoidance: Nietzsche and Libertarian Jurisprudence*, J. Juris. 321 (2014).

2 Richard Hammer, *The Helmsleys: The Rise and Fall of Harry and Leona* (New York: NAL Books, 1990).

3 Laureen Snider, *Theft of Time: Disciplining Through Science and Law*, 40 Osgoode Hall L. J. 89, 90 (2002) ("Corporations were to be viewed as complicated organisms run by well-intentioned, well-educated management teams. Harmful acts in which they might—accidentally, of course—engage were better handled by gentle persuasion or education rather than by arrest and prosecution.").

4 See Jeffrey A. Schoenblum, *Tax Fairness or Unfairness? A Consideration of the Philosophical Bases for Unequal Taxation of Individuals*, 12 Am. J. Tax Pol'y 221 (1995).

5 Richard Posner, *Utilitarianism, Economics, and Legal Theory*, 8 J. Legal Stud. 103 (1979); but see Ronald Dworkin, *Is Wealth a Value?* 9 J. Legal Stud. 191 (1980).

6 John Rawls, *Political Liberalism* (New York: Columbia University Press, 1986); Linda Sugin, *Theories of Distributive Justice and Limitations on Taxation: What Rawls Demands From Tax Systems*, 72 Fordham L. Rev. 1991, 1994 (2004); Rojhat B. Avsar, *A Rawlsian Defense of the Individual Mandate: The "Collective Asset" Approach*, 73 Rev. Soc. Econ. 146, 152 (2015); Geoffrey P. Miller, *Economic Efficiency and the Lockean Proviso*, 10 Harv. J.L. & Pub. Pol'y 401 (1987); Robert Nozick, *Anarchy, State, and Utopia* (New York: Basic Books, 1974); Jennifer Bird-Pollan, *Death, Taxes, and Property (Rights): Nozick, Libertarianism, and the Estate Tax*, 66 Maine L. Rev. 1 (2013).

7 *See* Bret N. Bogenschneider, *Manufactured Factual Indeterminacy and the Globalization of Tax Jurisprudence*, 4:2 Univ. College London J. Law & Juris. 250 (2015).

8 *See Parker v. Comm'r*, 724 F.2d 469, 471–72 (1984).

9 SSRS Polling Data and Results (Oct. 12–15, 2017), http://i2.cdn.turner.com/cnn/2017/images/10/17/rel10c_taxes.pdf CNN poll: Most Americans oppose Trump's tax reform plan, www.cnn.com/2017/10/18/politics/poll-trump-tax-reform/index.html ("Overall, do you favor or oppose the tax reform proposals made by the Trump administration? […] Favor: 34% Oppose: 52% No Opinion: 14%").

10 See Richard Rorty, *Philosophy and the Mirror of Nature* (Princeton, NJ: Princeton University Press, 1979); Bret N. Bogenschneider, *A Philosophy Toolkit for Tax Lawyers*, 50:3 Akron L. Rev. 451 (2017) ("Hence, agreement-in-use for language was always local and there would be no objectively given idea that could be valid in every possible context. Rorty argued that it would be impossible to know what future contexts would look like. Under this view, all debates, including that of law and taxation, are but of a larger conversation among mankind that could go in any direction. Habermas disagreed with Rorty on the point of the edifying use of language and argued that there exists practical usages of language, which are universally valid."). See also Jürgen Habermas, *Richard Rorty's Pragmatic Turn, in "Rorty and His Critics"* (Oxford: Blackwell, 2000), at 49.

11 Martin Feldstein, *Tax Avoidance and the Deadweight Loss of the Income Tax*, 81:4 Rev. Econ. & Stat. 674 (1999).

12 Bret N. Bogenschneider & Ruth Heilmeier, *Income Elasticity and Inequality*, 5:1 Int. J. Econ. & Bus. Law 34 (2016).

13 *The Growing Gap in Life Expectancy by Income: Implications for Federal Programs and Policy Responses* (Washington, DC: National Academies of Science Press, 2015), at 68 ("Thus, [in the U.S. social security system] there is no perception of unfairness,

and no distortion of decisions about labor supply."), http://www.nap.edu/19015. Accessed Nov. 10, 2015.

14 Nearly all tax research considers taxes harmful, except a line of research dealing with "sin" products such as tobacco and sugar-sweetened beverages, for which taxes are taken as helpful to the person required to pay them. See, e.g., K. Brownell et al., *The Public Health and Economic Benefits of Taxing Sugar-Sweetened Beverages*, 361 N. ENGL. J. MED. 1599 (2009).

15 Elisabeth Buchwald, *Why Aren't Most Americans Rich? These Theories May Help Explain It* (Oct. 20, 2018), https://www.marketwatch.com/story/why-arent-most-americans-rich-these-theories-may-help-explain-it-2018-07-02. Accessed Nov. 10, 2019.

INDEX